The Fundamentals of Insurance Marketing

Manuel Leiria

www.insurancemarketing-thebook.com

Copyright © 2016 by Manuel Leiria

All rights reserved.

No part of this publication may be reproduced, distributed, or transmitted in any form or by any means, without the prior written permission of the author, except in the case of non-commercial uses permitted by copyright law. For permission requests, write to the author (manuel.m.leiria@gmail.com).

Preface

This interesting, profound and original work on the marketing of insurance should be recommended as an excellent source of information in schools of Management and Marketing. The book characterizes the behaviour of customers who make decisions and how insurance companies must manage them in order to increase their value and retain them.

Insurance is one of the most important drivers for economic and social development of societies worldwide. The origin of insurance goes back to many centuries ago. Although it has been taking new forms, covering more and new risks over time, its central role of protection of goods and people is unchanged since then.

Nowadays, considering the intense competition among insurance companies and the new risks that emerge in our societies, insurance companies have to be more and more innovative and creative to be successful. In this environment, the marketing function plays a decisive role, providing the essential tools to improve the value of customers and hence the value of the insurance companies. Manuel Leiria explains in a simple and rigorous way how the modern marketing must be managed to increase the competitiveness of insurance companies, in this highly recommendable book.

Rui Leão Martinho

President of Insurance Portuguese Authority

Member of the Board of "The Geneva Association" (www.genevaassociation.org)

Prologue

A new book about insurance is always good news, mainly because there is a shortage of publications about this subject. The reason to the scarce production of these literary works lies in the lack of systematization as a scientific field of research.

The majority of the publications about insurance are focused in laws and regulation (following the tradition of Pedro de Santarém and his treatise on insurance) and also in actuarial sciences. However, these are usually very limited in quantity and scope.

"The fundamentals of Insurance Marketing" is certainly one of the most well organized books that details the importance of marketing to the insurance business, in a very ample and systematized way, especially in what concerns the positioning of insurers.

It's obvious to me that the success of insurance companies is closely related to the rules identified in this book: products and services with a high level of simplicity, efficient management of distribution channels, cautious management of sales networks, intelligent information systems, critical evaluation of customer satisfaction, organizational processes based on the immediate problem solving and the efficient management of insurable risks.

This book is an instrument of great value both to insurance professionals and citizens seeking to better understand the insurance industry, considering its methodology, the depth of the analysis and the ability to transmit knowledge in a simple, accessible and very comprehensive.

Pedro Seixas Vale

Chairman of Association of insurance and reinsurance companies operating in Portugal.

Preamble

This book of Manuel Leiria explores the insurance business and its main systems, and details the application of marketing tools to assist in the creation and development of distinctive value propositions.

Insurers have a key role in modern societies, both in preventing and mitigating the various risks, and in the collection and allocation of financial resources, thus contributing to the social development and wealth creation.

This book highlights the importance of tactics and how the marketing strategies should be implemented. In fact, for the success of any strategy, it is crucial to execute it properly. Despite the importance of a correct formulation of strategy, the art of management is the ability to implement it better and faster than competitors.

According to Manuel Leiria, business models evolve dynamically depending basically on the Company's strategy (the business model serves and follows the strategy) and on the changes imposed by the evolution of internal and external circumstances. The business model should have the vitality and elasticity to facilitate their tactical adaptation and the rapid incorporation of changes by commercial agents, without jeopardizing the strategy execution and the accomplishment of the insurer's objectives. A book about management, marketing and strategy, like this one, should not intend to be a dogma but a way to improve the comprehension of organizations and its mechanisms of evaluation and decision. This book of Manuel Leiria meets that objective, making it an excellent decision support tool.

Artur Marques

President of Atlas Insurance

Contents

Preface 3
Prologue 4
Preamble 5
Contents 6
List of Figures 8
List of Equations 10
1) Marketing management in the insurance sector 11
2) Marketing philosophies 13
    2A) Creating value for the community 14
    2B) Generating and maintaining trust 17
3) The insurance customer: Purchase decision process 19
    3A) Customer decision models 20
    3B) Customer involvement 24
    3C) Insurance purchase process 29
    3D) Recognition of the need for insurance 30
    3E) The information required for making a decision 38
    3 F) Assessing alternatives and decisions 49
    3G) Customer limitations in their ability to assess alternatives .. 53
    3H) Application of rules of decision 55
    3I) Neuromarketing 58
    3J) The particularities of collective customers 61
4) Managing the insurance customer 64
    4A) Customer knowledge 65
    4B) Development of the customer base 109
5) Marketing Plan 123

- 5A) Business strategy and tactics 124
- 5B) Strategy definition 133
- 5C) Monitoring the competition 138
- 5D) The fundamental metrics of marketing projects 141

6) Marketing strategies in the insurance sector 144
- 6A) Customer segmentation 146
- 6B) Target selection 159
- 6C) Positioning 159

7) Marketing tactics in the insurance sector 163
- 7A) The insurance product 164
- 7B) Price definition 172
- 7C) Insurance distribution 188
- 7D) Communication in insurance 212
- 7E) Complementary variables of the insurance marketing-mix .. 223
- 7F) Specific features of the insurance marketing-mix 230
- 7G) The brand 234

8) Marketing Information Systems 247
- 8A) Fundamental customer data 250
- 8B) Customer data management 252
- 8C) Technological infrastructure 254

9) The social media 256
- 9A) Social media: an inevitable reality 257
- 9B) Principal forms of social media 260
- 9C) Insurance in social media 264
- 9D) Monitoring presence in the social media 269

Bibliographical references 272
About the Author 278

List of Figures

Figure 1: Marketing concepts 13
Figure 2: The scope of customer analysis 19
Figure 3: Explanatory models of customer behaviour 21
Figure 4: Decision process for the purchase of Insurance 30
Figure 5: Sources of external information 40
Figure 6: Relationship between the type of decision and evoked brands 47
Figure 7: Customer rules of decision 55
Figure 8: Phases of the customer management process 65
Figure 9: Summary-table for strategic approach to customer segments 72
Figure 10: Strategic customer management indicators 74
Figure 11: Process of analysing customer satisfaction 77
Figure 12: Simplified model for determining satisfaction 85
Figure 13: Priority areas of intervention, based on the customer satisfaction 87
Figure 14 Key moments in customer experience management 90
Figure 15 Basic points of contact between insurers and their customers 94
Figure 16: Monitoring the perceived quality of experiences 97
Figure 17: The process of customer retention 115
Figure 18: The process of increasing customer value 117
Figure 19: Process of marketing planning 124
Figure 20: Defining the strategic "where" 127
Figure 21: The attractiveness of the market segments 134
Figure 22: Map of insurer competitive position within the critical success factors 134
Figure 23: Illustrative maps of segments and distribution channels 137
Figure 24: Illustrative representation of strategic priorities in the binomial "segment/channel" 138

Figure 25: Simplified characterisation of competitors 140

Figure 26: Marketing as a means of value creation 144

Figure 27: Model of value creation 145

Figure 28: Segmentation criteria 147

Figure 29: Phases in the life cycle of families 150

Figure 30: Illustrative segmentation matrix resulting from crossing value and family life cycle 156

Figure 31: Segmentation matrix resulting from customer value and distribution channel 156

Figure 32: Basis for the development of individual customer segmentation 158

Figure 33: Basis for the development of business customer segmentation 158

Figure 34: Positioning options 160

Figure 35: The three dimensions of the insurance product 171

Figure 36: Reasons for increasing or lowering premiums 183

Figure 37: Distribution channels 188

Figure 38: Effect of distribution channel on other marketing variables 195

Figure 39: Impact of partnership agreements with agents, brokers and banks 197

Figure 40: Communication targets 215

Figure 41: Means of communication 216

Figure 42: Positive and negative associations of different colours 218

Figure 43: "Deep Diving" task process 228

Figure 44: Specific features of insurance marketing-mix 231

Figure 45: Central Aspects of insurance brand management 241

Figure 46: Models of brand architecture 243

List of Equations

Equation 1: Simple calculation of customer value 66

Equation 2: Adapted calculation of customer value 67

Equation 3: Insurance customer value with adapted assumptions 69

Equation 4: Quantification of the competitive position................................. 135

Equation 5: Pure premium calculation.. 179

1) Marketing management in the insurance sector

Insurance plays a fundamental role in the economic and social development of contemporary communities. The well-being of individuals and corporate progress would not be guaranteed without insurance.

The mission of insurance marketing consists of:

- developing initiatives that position the insurance company as a profitable and competitive organisation;
- ensuring maximum value for entities dealing with the insurer and for the community in which it operates.

Insurance company marketing needs to grow from a fragmented operation, focused on short term challenges, into a structure that identifies the best customers and intermediaries with which to do business. It must establish priorities for developing the insurance company, which include:

- creating alternative means of increasing value to the entire ecosystem;
- improving experiences offered to customers and intermediaries;
- re-thinking the insurer's business models to make them right for current day competitive challenges.

Marketing allows insurers to meet major current day management challenges by reconciling the consistent increase in value for customers, employees, shareholders and society as a whole with the insurer's own competitive strength.

The insurer's success depends greatly on its ability to increase the value of its main asset – the customer. As with other company assets, customers must be managed and valued.

The insurer must be aware of the value of each customer so that it can attract and retain those that are most valuable. As with other corporate assets, future customer value can be forecast. The ability to identify and invest in those likely to be of greater value depends on the amount and quality of information that the insurer has on its customers. The first challenge for insurance marketing success is to understand the importance of this information.

Improving the insurer's analytical abilities by providing its employees with the best technical and scientific training and making the most of technological developments in the field of competitive intelligence, has led to insurers being more aggressive in attracting and retaining profitable customers.

Customers are less loyal in their relationship with insurers when:

- they are better informed and more aware of how the insurance market works;

- the environmental framework is more open and less regulated, encouraging the entry of new competitors that adopt more innovative tactics than those pursued by existing insurance companies.

In the past, the response to the great environmental and social challenges, which turned into marketing challenges, came through investing in mass communication. Today these solutions are far less effective. To a large extent, insurer success is achieved by reviewing the circumstances, moments and locations in which customer interaction takes place. Gradually improving the approach to customer contact, and particularly the insurer-customer relationship, has become a critical success factor.

The paradigm of contemporary insurance marketing consists of knowing and understanding the entities the insurance company is dealing with in order to build mutually beneficial relationships.

2) Marketing philosophies

Marketing, as a management philosophy, puts the customer first, in an environment where priorities are determined by external variables. The insurer's role is to come up with better solutions than those of its competitors in order to meet the needs of those involved in its economic and social role. Two complementary concepts are deduced from this marketing perspective:

- Companies direct their approach according to rules dictated by the market, to the detriment of the company's own dictates. This philosophy must be incorporated into company culture to serve as a guide to employees so that they can perform their tasks accordingly.

- It is an organizational function responsible for defining both the insurer's position and the measures that lead to its competitive success.

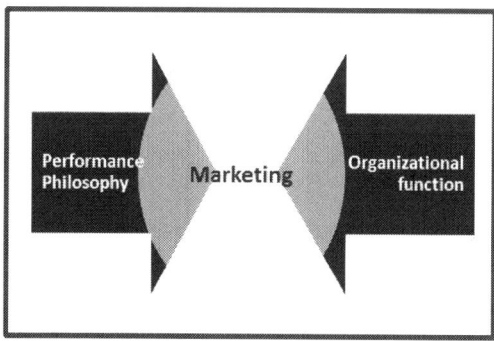

Figure 1: Marketing concepts

The two dimensions are equally important for the success of business organisations, which need to generate profit in order to survive.

Another way of clarifying the concept is to indicate what is not marketing. Marketing should not be confused with:

- Advertising and promotion. Although these are two components of the marketing process, in fact the best known because they deal directly with brand image, they are no more than two marketing tools.

- Hard selling, or the commercial exploitation of customers by companies. This is an out-dated marketing approach, although it is still practised in the insurance sector. Here the company's priority is to maximise sales, within the shortest timeframe and at the highest possible price. Although this approach may generate good results in the present, it puts a burden on the company's future capacity for business development.

- Market studies. This is another very important and popular component of the marketing process and perhaps one of the areas where the scientific component is most revealed, but it is no more than a phase in the marketing process.

So contemporary marketing operates on the principle of creating value for the community and establishing a trustworthy environment for the parties concerned.

Customer value management is a central marketing management tool because it determines the Insurer's success. The main financial flow that allows companies to pay their own costs, invest in new solutions, distribute dividends to shareholders and to meet their social obligations, is generated by the premiums paid by its customers. It is essential that all employees, regardless of their duties and responsibilities, share this marketing culture, given that they all have an impact on the customers' perception of the value generated by the Insurer.

2A) Creating value for the community

The insurers' image is not as good as one would hope. Although some studies show that customer satisfaction rating is positive, many customers do not enjoy a trusting relationship with their insurance company and they do not recognise the vital economic and social role that the Insurer plays.

Societies in developed countries find insurers relatively indifferent, disinterested and even oblivious to the social, economic and environmental problems of the communities in which they operate, in that they do not get sufficiently involved in solving social problems. However, paradoxically, resources invested by insurers in philanthropic and social solidarity causes are on the rise.

The increase in philanthropic costs can be counter-productive if they affect the Insurer's competitiveness and consequently limit its risk management ability.

Philanthropy plays a smaller role in the insurer's involvement in social and economic activities when compared to the added value it creates for its shareholders, customers, employees and partners.

Contemporary marketing has to deal differently with the insurer's environmental liabilities.

The approach to new marketing is to create social value in the same way that economic value is created: including social impact as one of the decisive criteria for assessing interest. This concern must be rooted within the organisational culture of the insurance company. The following examples classify this organisational development concept:

- not selling products carrying exclusions that customers only become aware of after they have made a claim;

- including in all insurance documentation the warranties that ensure a minimum level of basic safety: customers may not be aware of the potential impact of not being safeguarded against the occurrence of basic risks;

- not accepting contracts with a significantly lower sum insured than that of the value of the insured goods or assets;

- not cancelling contracts due to an excess of claims made, in particular when such claims are not caused by careless or irresponsible customer behaviour, and in particular when the type of insurance covers personal risks and for which alternatives would be difficult to come by.

Society recognises and distinguishes insurers that adopt an attitude compatible with the marketing philosophy and that create value for the community.

We are not focusing on the "ethical customer", who prefers to pay more for an insurance that supports a social cause rather than pay for a cheaper insurance not associated with any cause at all. Experience in developing insurance specific to the "ethical customer" has not produced satisfactory results. This is because customers who purchase more expensive products because of their association with social causes form a niche market, far too small to generate a positive return on investment.

However, customers heavily penalise insurers that do not respect the fundamental principles of business ethics. For this reason, the Insurer's ethical behaviour should be duly explained:

- to those in some way related to the insurer;

- by insurer associations, emphasising the social and economic importance of insurance and its irreplaceable role in the balance and development of the communities in which it operates.

One of the most pressing marketing challenges consists of striking a balance between the benefits allocated to the different entities in some way related to the insurer. If one party receives too many benefits, there will be fewer benefits for others.

If, for example, the company chooses to make a significant increase in benefits to customers, it will reduce its capacity to pay employees, remunerate shareholders and to share its results with the social environment of which it is part. If, however, it chooses to distribute more dividends to shareholders, it will decrease its capacity to invest in the insurance company itself. If it chooses to assign no relevant contribution to society, it will affect other parties by reducing intangible benefits indirectly attributed to them:

- in the case of customers, who will realise that social responsibility is inadequate;
- in the case of employees, by reducing the feeling of belonging;
- in the case of shareholders, by the responsibility of having share capital in a company that is insensitive to surrounding social issues.

2B) Generating and maintaining trust

Given that the insurance product provides an undertaking that, should any event occur, the insurer will respond rapidly, diligently and predictably, there must be mutual trust between the parties involved in the business.

A determining factor in a company's ability to do business, to hire and retain the best employees, to develop and retain a distribution network, is its trustworthiness. There is a direct relationship between the trust placed in the insurance company and that company's current and future value.

Economic crises, particularly that affecting the financial sector, as well as frequent reports on scandals and fraud in leading companies, has generated a decline in customer confidence in the financial, banking and insurance sectors. This phenomenon has been further exacerbated by the fact that society views companies as having increased social responsibilities, which follows immediately with the perception that such new responsibilities have not been fully recognised or undertaken.

Trust is an intangible company asset. It takes a long time to build up, and yet it can be lost in an instant. The fragility of this asset has increased even more with the development of social networks. In this environment, a customer that is not satisfied with a given insurance company may cause severe damage to its image and reputation, undermining trust, regardless of how fair that customer's discontent really is.

One major approach for an insurance company to maintain a high level of trust is to be cautious in everything it says and does. The determining factors for this caution are:

- employee training, so as to ensure employees are prepared to answer queries clearly, and when they are not sure of an answer to find someone immediately to clear up doubts, whether responding to end customers or agents.

- reliably obtaining, handling and processing customer information and converting it into measures that meet the company's requirements, and those of its agents.

The attitude, knowledge and culture of those involved are essential in avoiding mistakes due to carelessness or ignorance, and this minimises any grounds for suspicion.

The loss of confidence in a company can affect trust throughout the entire industry, in the same way that the degree of confidence in an industry affects trust in all companies within that business sector.

As with all other relevant assets of the insurance company, confidence levels must be monitored, quantified and the determining factors measured, in particular through:

- surveys with those in some way related to the insurer;

- analysis of indirect confidence indicators, available to insurers, such as complaints or purchase recall.

3) The insurance customer: Purchase decision process

By studying customer behaviour we can analyse how customers spend their available resources (time, money and effort) on the insurance purchase, and it features:

- what customers buy (what type of insurance and at what price), in order to develop solutions that meet the current and potential needs of the different segments;

- why they buy, determining the customer's needs and reasoning in purchasing an insurance solution. This understanding makes insurers more effective in meeting these needs and, at the same time, in developing attractive solutions for non-customers;

- where they buy, in order to make the insurance available to customers in the most convenient places. The insurance business is characterised by the fact that different types of insurance are purchased, preferably, through certain distribution channels;

- purchasing frequency, crucial in identifying the moment at which

    o customers are more vulnerable to competitor offers, emphasising the importance of managing contract renewal;
    o initiatives to attract customers away from competing insurers should be triggered.

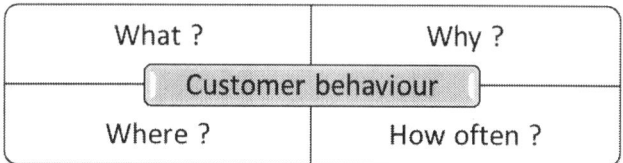

Figure 2: The scope of customer analysis

The study of customer behaviour demands very comprehensive insurer marketing abilities and qualifications. We need to understand the factors influencing the adoption of certain behaviour patterns, and this involves psychology, sociology, management, economics, statistics and marketing.

Knowledge of the insurance purchasing decision process allows insurance companies to determine the most appropriate approach for each of its customer segments, namely:

- the features of the best solution;
- the most suitable prices;
- the places where customers want to purchase these;
- the way in which a message and its content is used in communication.

Individual customer studies are more complex than those of collective studies. The decision process within companies is more standardised and is generally subject to several filters, opinions and assessments provided by the different participants in the company's value chain.

Contrary to what happens with individuals, company decision makers are accountable to other entities for the choices made, and this demands that a more rational decision be taken.

Analysis of purchasing processes, set out below, is based on individual and family behaviour. The final part of the chapter describes the main features of decision-making processes within companies.

3A) Customer decision models

The study of customer behaviour has evolved from various sciences (economics, psychology, sociology and business management), highlighting the different aspects, depending on the area under study.

The decision-making process of an individual customer is very unpredictable because it depends on the actual customer and that customer's circumstances. There are physical and psychological constraints in an individual's life that cannot be estimated or anticipated, therefore the behaviour of the individual customer is very difficult to explain, and consequently difficult to predict or anticipate.

However, there is a series of scientific models used in research into customer behaviour, and this allow us to predict that in a given situation a customer with certain characteristics, not subjected to other constraints, will tend to adopt a certain behaviour.

In this context, the main theories that aim to explain customer behaviour are based on economic, passive, emotional and cognitive models.

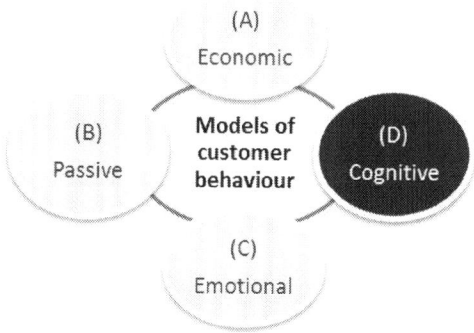

Figure 3: Explanatory models of customer behaviour

3A1) Economic model

Developments in economic theory have been important for the study of customer behaviour. However, by tradition, the assumption is that there are individuals who make rational decisions in order to maximise use and/or satisfaction. The assumption is that the customer is aware of all existing alternatives and is able to compare and evaluate them in order to make a final selection and buy the best possible solution.

In effect, the grounds for this model do not fully correspond to reality, in that:

- customers do make irrational decisions because they do not look to maximising use of the product. The reason for making the purchase may be linked to emotions and feelings associated with the purchase process or being in possession of an insurance;

- customers are not aware of, nor is it possible for them to be aware of, all types of insurance;

- the vast majority of customers do not have the necessary resources or knowledge to be able to compare and evaluate all types of insurance adequately;

- customers do not proceed to purchase until they find the best solution. There is a point at which they consider that the additional effort and costs incurred in searching for a better solution than the current one, are not compensated by the increased benefits to be had in acquiring a more perfect solution.

For these reasons, the economic model is not the best for explaining customer behaviour.

3A2) Passive model

The passive model assumes that a customer is influenced by the techniques developed by specialists in the manipulation of human behaviour. This concept dates back to the period in which it was argued that the aim of marketing was to sell as much as possible in the shortest possible timeframe, at the highest possible price, regardless of the satisfaction of customers or agents.

In this approach, customers are characterised as being naturally impulsive and irrational, purchasing products irrespective of needs or usefulness, when subjected to marketing and/or promotional campaigns.

Although customers show signs of some irrational behaviour and of being influenced by purchase incentives, in the majority of cases they tend to adopt more rational behaviour and are not completely vulnerable to marketing incentives. In addition, there are other legal and regulatory customer defence instruments that protect customers from those who adopt these less transparent and ethical approaches.

In conclusion, this model scarcely adheres to daily reality as it is not a key in explaining customer behaviour.

3A3) Emotional model

Out of the four approaches presented, the emotional model is the most recent and also the one that explains the phenomena better than other theories. In this model, the customer's decision is associated with feelings and deep emotions, some positive (such as security, joy, love, hope or imagination) and some negative (such as risk, fear or anxiety).

Decisions are strongly conditioned by impulse and emotion, with less importance attached to rational procedures that are based on detailed, valid information on what insurance is available. Customers purchase the products because of the feelings associated with the process of acquiring the item, possessing it and its anticipated use.

3A4) Cognitive model

This is the most appropriate, accepted and used model for explaining how customers make their decisions.

The customer reacts to becoming aware of the need to consume in purchasing an insurance, which may not be the best choice, but which maximises the cost/effort ratio spent in the purchase process and in finding the right insurance.

The exception to this rule is when the purchase process gives the customer a positive, pleasant and favourable feeling. In such cases, even when there is no

- a personal connection with an employee, such as a family member working at the insurance company;

- identifying with certain values. For example, *Zurich* personifies the stability and strength of the Swiss Confederation, while *Liberty* positions itself around the values of an *"American way of life"*.

- historical and geographical roots, such as *Açoreana* Insurance company, which emerged in the Azores in 1892;

- being linked to a social, cultural or sporting activity with significant meaning for the customer, such as the Formula 1 sponsorship by *Allianz*.

Normally, when there are close ties with the insurance company, there is less involvement in the purchasing process, given that a search for alternatives is not required.

Customers who have suffered a loss or made a claim, and were satisfied with the way the process was handled, are more likely to repurchase and recommend the brand to others. However, if we consider that over 80% of customers have never suffered a loss and that fewer than 5% have ever made a claim, then we can conclude that other procedures involving customer interaction should also be carefully monitored.

Purchasing as a routine

In habitual purchases, and contrary to purchases made by loyal customers, there is no involvement with the insurance or the insurer.

The customer believes that the existing alternatives to such insurance are very similar to those it already purchases and for this reason sees no advantages to justify the effort of searching and assessing additional solutions. And so the individual purchases the same insurance, normally from the same sales outlet.

Having purchased the insurance, and provided there is no unsatisfactory experience, when the same need comes to be renewed, the purchase is repeated with the same brand and from the same sales outlet.

Since the customer does not become involved with the brand or the product, there is also no involvement in the process, which leaves them vulnerable to initiatives by competitors. For example, if there is a promotional offer at the sales office, the customer will develop a limited decision process, in which a more detailed analysis is then made of the alternatives, comparing the advantages and disadvantages of each option and then making the customer more liable to change from the usual choice.

In certain circumstances, and with certain types of insurance (such as travel insurance), choice is less related to the characteristics of the insurance or the insurer itself, but more associated with the location of the sales office.

The following examples of insurance purchase show how this choice model is applied:

- for many years when travelling by plane, I would buy my travel insurance at an automatic vending machine at the airport. I only did so because I believed that the benefit gained from purchasing the insurance in any other location would not be worth the additional effort; I had no preference for this particular brand of insurance or insurer, other than the convenience of the location of the vending machine.

- in most cases, purchasing insurance associated with bank loans does not involve any type of analysis, study, comparison or assessment by customers, given that it is a bank requirement for the purpose of acquiring something adding value for the customer, that is, the bank loan itself.

The vast majority of insurance purchase decisions is nominal and carried out as a matter of habit. In effect, more than half the decisions made in customer choice (on a global basis) take less than five seconds.

Studies into the reason for buying insurance in a given place show that one of the most common answers refers to "it's where my family usually buys".

3B2) Limited decisions

Limited decisions have an intermediate level of complexity. The information that the customer has is not enough to meet the customer's needs, therefore additional information will be sought to determine what options are available, how to assess and compare them and, in the end, to apply a simple decision criteria to choose which one to buy.

Insurance purchase decisions related to products with some complexity (such as, workers' compensation) have a tendency to become more limited. Customers turn to agents whom they consider qualified in the field, or they do some research (done increasingly via the internet), after which they assess whether the solution found matches their required characteristics and price. Should this be the case, the insurance is then purchased. If they are not satisfied with the alternative found, the process begins again, this time using a more extensive choice model.

3B3) Extensive choices

This method involves cases where the customer is very much involved with the purchase. The process is highly complex, time-consuming and detailed. Very few customer decisions are made using this amount of detail.

As soon as customers become aware of the need to purchase a given type of insurance, they carry out an extensive search for information to help in their selection, using their own personal sources (such as memory, experience and knowledge), and external sources. Following this, a detailed assessment is made of alternatives and a decision taken by applying a complex set of rules.

After purchasing the insurance, the customer carries out regular quality assessments of the insurance purchased.

Normally, the insurance purchase is not made using this degree of complexity. However, in given circumstances, as in the purchase of financial products, where savings made over many years are invested or where an asset of particular importance to the customer is sold, it is only natural that the process adopted by the customer will be more detailed.

3C) Insurance purchase process

The fundamental stages of the decision process in purchasing insurance are as follows (according to figure 4)[1]:

- the process starts as soon as the customer becomes aware of the need to purchase the insurance;

- the customer tries to find an insurance using (internal) information available. Information is sought in order to find out what insurances are available that meet requirements, how to make the purchase, how to assess and compare them;

- in a few cases, the internal information is insufficient, and the customer looks for external sources;

- once this information is available, the customer identifies alternatives;

- the customer compares insurances available with the factors determining the decision;

- the application of rules of decision identifies the best possible choice.

---

[1] Based on Hawkins, 1998; and Schiffman, 1997.

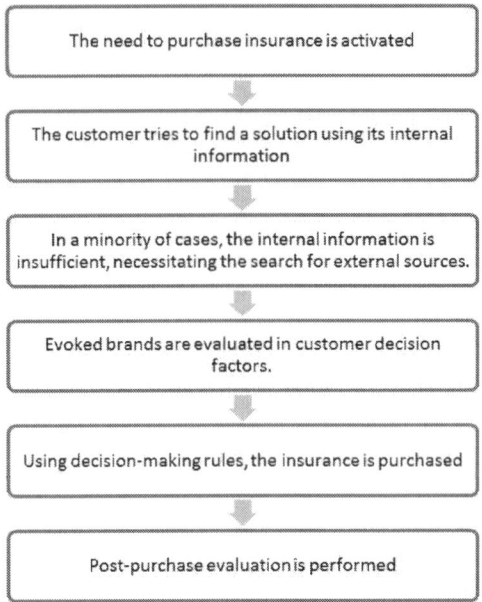

Figure 4: Decision process for the purchase of Insurance

3D) Recognition of the need for insurance

The four main reasons for acquiring insurance are as follows:

- Risk aversion. The customer believes that a loss arising from a possible event, taking into account the corresponding financial loss, is greater than the cost of the insurance premium, which eliminates or drastically reduces such a possibility.

- Legal obligation. There are a series of risks that legally demand insurance cover (which normally must have a fixed amount of insurance cover and minimum sums insured), i.e., in some countries, third party liability insurance, occupational accident insurance, hunting practices or insurance broker management.

- Contractual requirement. Several types of contract demand an insurance, in which, in the event of a claim, one of the parties is regarded as beneficiary or mortgage lender. Examples of these are life insurance or property all-risk insurance demanded by banks in lending mortgages for home purchase.

- Asset development. Financial life insurance and assurance (such as Retirement Savings Plans) compete directly with other financial applications in an attempt to get a hold of the customer's long-term savings.

However, these reasons may be associated with more or less obvious customer needs:

- some needs are immediately recognised, classified and resolved, such as those arising out of legal obligations or contractual requirements;

- other needs may not be as easily recognised and are therefore more difficult to resolve, such as agricultural, health or travel insurance;

- finally, there are customer needs, such as retirement savings plans, the recognition of which may take more time; these are more subtle and evolve over time, making them only truly resolved after a period of assessment and maturity.

When these different types of need arise, the insurer is faced with two types of challenge:

- identifying the need to purchase insurance;

- activating the need to purchase insurance;

- when necessary, suppressing acknowledgement of the need for insurance.

3D1) Activating the need to purchase insurance

All customers are subject to a wide variety of risks, which may affect them personally or affect their assets, and there is a permanent need to prevent such occurrences.

However, many of these needs are not active, given that, despite being real, the customer is not aware of their existence.

The awareness of the need to acquire insurance is only activated when the customer is aware of an important and strong enough discrepancy between existing status and some other status in which he or she wants or needs to be in.

This discrepancy may already exist in a latent form, however if it is not given due value or does not have the required intensity, it does not activate the process of insurance acquisition. As a rule of thumb, this need is not activated because the customer considers the likelihood of a claim, or its impact, to be low, which consequently generates a low intensity in the discrepancy.

In the case of motor insurance, the vast majority of customers purchase third party liability insurance; however, less than half of these customers purchase the optional cover for car theft or break-in. Although the discrepancy is important, given that the theft of a car has a potentially high impact, the likelihood of such a claim occurring is low, and as such its intensity is low.

Marketing approaches differ according to whether needs are active or inactive.

- in the first case, the insurer's priority is to convince customers that its offers will benefit them most;

- in the second case, customers must first be made aware of the need to acquire insurance, highlighting the risks to which they are exposed, as well as the potential consequences of a claim occurring, and only then can Insurers convince customers that their insurance is most beneficial.

One indicator that shows the effectiveness of insurance company marketing is the relative weight of non-mandatory insurance, given that before it can be sold the will to purchase must first be activated.

To activate the customer's need to purchase insurance the insurer has to know the types of risk to which each customer sector is exposed. The main techniques for this identification are:

- surveys and focus groups, through which customers and agents are questioned about the most relevant risks to which they are exposed, and those they value the most.

- activities analysis, which consists of identifying customer activities (professional and extra-professional), in order to determine the resulting risks;

- identifying risks customers are exposed to and against which they are insufficiently covered by existing offers, through identifying the insurance performance the customer already has, and that are marketed by brokerage companies.

Complaints are a good source for identifying product improvement opportunities for what is already on sale. Establishing the main sources of conflict in claims settlement also helps identify what needs to be improved in a particular offer.

Insurers may activate the customer's awareness of the need to purchase a given type of insurance by using generic or selective processes.

- Generic awareness causes an increase in the volume of business within the entire market, with each insurer increasing its sales in proportion to its share. For example, if the market grows by 5%, it is expected that an insurer with a 20% share, will increase its business turnover by 1% (assuming the principle that any other variables contributing towards sales are irrelevant).

This approach is usually implemented by business associations or by insurers that have a large market share, given that they are the ones that most benefit in terms of absolute value.

This initiative is justified when insurance needs are acknowledged to be latent and when:

- o the product is at an early stage in its life cycle;
- o after becoming aware of the problem, demand for external information is limited;
- o there is a concerted effort on behalf of the entire industry.

- Selective acknowledgement is based on the fact that an insurer is regarded as being the best, or one of the few, to meet a particular safety need, which contributes towards the growth of its market share. This approach does not contribute towards market growth, given that the growth of one insurance company is achieved by taking away value from other insurers.

In most cases there is in effect a fall in market value because the insurer that uses such a method, and those that defend it, aim to ensure customer preference through:

- o reducing the final premiums paid by customers;

- o maintaining prices, but with an increase in benefits to the customer, to the distribution channel or to both.

Whatever the case, the result will always lower insurer profits and market value.

Given that identifying customer needs is the result of identifying a discrepancy between the current customer state and desired state, activation is achieved by altering the perception of current state or desired state, or by increasing the intensity of the discrepancy.

The customer's current state can be altered by alerting customers to possible risks, for example:

- disseminating news and statistics on certain types of claims, such as shop burglaries;

- alerting customers to the consequences of allowing insurances, such as labour related accident insurance, to expire;

- highlighting the criminal consequences of not having certain compulsory insurance, such as insurance for to cover hunting.

The way customers perceive their current status is not always an objective reality, so that it is often determined using customer life style and existing status, among other factors:

- lifestyle represents the way in which customers choose to live, given the constraints imposed by the scarcity of resources;

- existing status, because it is strongly influenced by the almost immediate challenges and issues that customers have to deal with. It should be noted that a customer's existing status can be influenced by factors, such as:

    o their prior choices;

    o emotions;

    o governmental action or customer rights groups activities;

    o the availability of insurance that satisfies their needs.

The desired status can be influenced by advertising the benefits that insurances will generate in the hope that these benefits will be desirable to customers. The following examples show how to change the desired status of a customer:

- demonstrating how public system pension guarantees may not ensure the same level of income that customers have become accustomed to during their working life;

- to ensure, by means of funeral insurance, (which is a successful product in some European and South American countries) that the customer's funeral arrangements will correspond to their wishes, regardless of the will or financial surety of family and friends.

The desired status can be influenced by factors, such as:

- culture;

- reference groups;

- individual circumstances, regarding family, profession, finances and even emotions.

Regarding the importance of the discrepancy between current status and desired status, customers should be aware of the large probability of being affected by a given occurrence, and that in the event of such an occurrence, the consequences will have a serious impact on their personal well-being and assets.

If the magnitude of the discrepancy is low, the customer does not have sufficient reason to move towards the next stage of the decision process. The relative importance of each need is a critical factor in triggering the insurance purchase procedure.

The importance of each need is determined by the degree to which each customer problem may affect the continuation of the desired lifestyle.

The occurrence of serious claims constitutes an opportunity for insurers to demonstrate the importance of covering such risks, given that this perception may be crucial for customers to purchase fully comprehensive products, limiting the importance of the cost factor.

Activating awareness of the need to purchase some product types may raise ethical issues, in particular where issues concerning individual status or social acceptance are considered important. However, in the case of insurance this is not normally the case, given that:

- the act of purchasing or acquiring insurance does not usually change the customer's social status;

- the need for safety is essential;

- the alternative to acquiring insurance is self-assurance. This consists of customers taking upon themselves responsibility for the consequences of a claim arising out of events for which they are liable. This solution is usually more harmful for both the customer and society than transferring the risk to an insurer.

3D2) Suppressing the acknowledgment of a customer need

In certain circumstances, insurers may prefer to suppress the customer's acknowledgement of the need to purchase insurance, particularly in the following situations:

- some insurance brands whose insurances are purchased based on nominal or limited decisions, prefer customers not to be made aware of existing competing products with more comprehensive cover;

- the existence of insufficiently covered risks, but for which the insurer does not have a solution to meet such customer needs, as in the following examples:

- earthquake cover is a necessity often not fully covered under property insurance. However, insurers do not make a significant effort to promote its marketing, especially in geographical areas where there is greater risk of seismic activity.

- unlimited motor liability insurance is a customer need that was suppressed due to no reinsurance cover being available.

3E) The information required for making a decision

Finding information right for customer decision-making is an on-going process. Customers always recognise where there are needs and opportunities. However, customers actively seeking information and ready to interact with insurers before committing to their purchases should be distinguished from those who are not prepared to make any effort at all to understand available solutions.

There is a physical and psychological cost to customers who obtain information that improves the quality of a decision, for example, the loss of time accessing sources of information rather than spending time on more enjoyable activities. This is why the search will only take place when the customer perceives that the benefits will outweigh the loss.

However, a significant portion of information required for the right customer decision is obtained without a search. This is acquired as low involvement learning that goes on throughout the life of the customer.

3E1) Sources of customer information

In response to the need to acquire insurance, customers resort to using their past experiences, memory and low involvement learning in an attempt to identify a satisfactory solution that will allow them to meet this need, as well as in applying their approach to comparing those options.

In most customer cases, the primary source used by customers is their own inside information. Customer memory accumulates information previously obtained via external sources.

In cases where customers consider their inside information is insufficient to make a decision, they turn to external sources, in particular:

- people who are close to them, such as friends, neighbours, relatives or colleagues, and above all those they consider to have special knowledge and skill in the subject;

- commercial networks of insurers and distributors;

- information from independent origins, such as that provided by customer associations and government organisations;

- technical data available in reports, studies, books and articles;

- direct experience, as a result of testing and product experimentation promoted by the supplier (see 4B1 – Testing the experience);

- insurer advertising, such as flyers, brochures, ads, promotions and sales force.

- the Internet, increasingly the preferred channel for obtaining information, namely through insurance related and risk management web sites, insurance company sites, social networks and also aggregators. In the latter case, ratings, rankings and comments are of particular relevance in forming customer preferences.

The Internet has become the most popular way of obtaining information. The majority of communication campaigns conducted by insurers involve this environment, particularly to highlight messages that are not eligible for publication through traditional channels.

The ZMOT (zero moment of truth) concept refers to the search for the information with online tools, such as: search engine, aggregator, insurance company website or customer reviews.

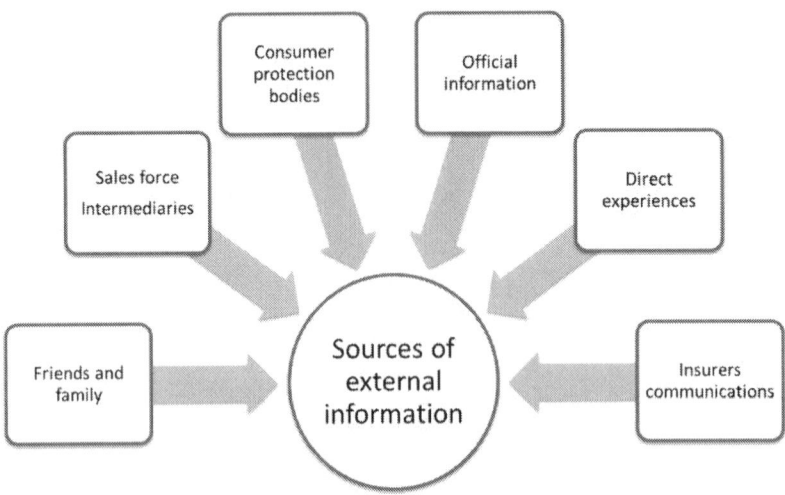

Figure 5: Sources of external information

The relative importance of each source varies according to the category of insurance. However, marketing activities influence all other sources, and these are often designed to have an impact on decision makers, when these differ from customers. On the other hand, the fact that the act of purchasing insurance is predominantly nominal in nature, to a large extent explains why, in many countries, agents and brokers are the preferred channel for purchasing non-life insurance and banks are preferred for the distribution of life insurance.

The search for information can also occur in the absence of a need to acquire insurance; this happens for two reasons:

- the customer prefers, or enjoys, conducting the search;
- the social reward from sharing the knowledge that results from such a search.

3E2) The amount of researched information

Customers search to obtain information to help them make a satisfactory decision. The search has costs and benefits, and consequently customers cease to look for information when they realise that gains to be made from such additional information are less than the benefits drawn from a more accurate and reasoned decision.

The benefits associated with the search for information can be classified as:

- tangible, when the search leads to achieving a quantifiable benefit, such as obtaining a lower price, a better combination of cover or a reduction in charges;

- intangible, when the result of the search generates benefits that cannot be measured, such as reducing the risk of an insurer not fulfilling its commitments.

On the other hand, the costs associated with searching for external information are:

- monetary, such as travel costs or the acquisition of documents;

- non-monetary, physical and psychological costs, such as tiredness, fatigue or frustration from being prevented from enjoying other activities.

Even if the non-monetary costs are less obvious, they can be more important for the customer than monetary costs when considering the cost-benefit associated with the process of searching for external information.

There are factors associated with market features, types of insurance, the actual customer and the circumstances in which the purchase is made, all of which affect the way in which the costs and benefits of the search information are perceived. Each customer makes an individual assessment of the costs and benefits associated with purchasing the same type of insurance, which explains why some customers search for external information and others do not.

The following market factors increase the amount of external information sought by customers:

- the existence of many options;

- a wide range of prices between the various existing insurances;

- the number of sales outlets, those closer and more conveniently located;

- the quantity and diversity of information available.

The following insurance characteristics also influence the amount of external information sought by customers:

- the higher the price, the more information researched;

- the greater the difference between insurances, the more information researched;

- for 'positive' insurance policies that generate good feelings and emotions, such as setting up a pension plan, more information is researched than for negative insurance policies, the function of which is to minimize or eliminate an unpleasant feeling or condition, the case of insurance cover for a serious illnesses.

The characteristics of customers themselves are also associated with the amount of external information researched:

- prior positive insurance experiences reduce the need to search for additional information;

- middle class society tends to search for more information than the upper or lower classes;

- in the case of adults, the older the customer, the less the demand for information;

- the greater the risk associated with the purchase, the more information sought.

Lastly, there are factors related to circumstances at the time of purchase that affect the amount of information sought, in particular:

- the time factor is likely to be the most important circumstantial factor in the amount of information being sought, as there is a direct relationship between the two factors (time and in-depth search);

- the status of the customer also affects the amount of information being sought, for example, less information is sought if the person's physical or emotional energy is low;

- a pleasant physical environment and the existence of friendly and efficient staff at a sales office, tend to increase the search for information.

3E3) The type of information being sought

Customers require information that allows them to:

- identify the characteristics required in each insurance;

- know the types of insurance available;

- determine the performance of the available insurance products in response to customer needs.

Customers need to know the characteristics of the insurance to ensure their needs are adequately met. These characteristics can be:

- exogenous to the insurance - such as the insurer's reputation, the proximity of the sales office or the diligence and professionalism of the agent.

- endogenous to the insurance - associated with the way in which it was designed, formatted and made available, that is, the combination of coverage, deductibles, price, exclusions, waiting periods, service networks or co-payments.

However, the customer identifies a limited set of factors, usually three to five, which are the most important in adapting the insurance to needs. The choice of insurance is not based on an assessment of each product as a whole, but from comparing the performance of the insurance with those factors that are of utmost importance to the customer.

When acquiring financial insurance, it is natural for customers to pay particular attention to the rate, charges, timeframe or solidity of the insurer. For the acquisition of motor insurance, the most relevant factors are different, such as, cover, deductibles, price or the insurer's reputation when it comes to settling claims.

The desired characteristics are therefore the assessment criteria used by the customer. The search for information is required at an initial stage for the customer to determine the assessment criteria to be used in decision-making.

Both customer associations and insurers provide information to influence the assessment criteria used by customers. The former aims to improve the quality of the customer's decision, the latter aims to match the criteria used with its own competitive strengths.

In getting to know the types of insurance available, very few customers search for external information, as the majority of decisions are nominal or limited.

The increased financial literacy of customers and ease of access to information has brought about an information search pattern that is essentially characterised by:

- more and more purchases are made after visiting a sales office;

- in most situations, the search focuses on just one brand and one option;

- the customer mainly contacts its own personal sources;

- specialised studies or reports by customer organisations are rarely consulted.

3E4) The options considered

After, and often during the process of determining their decision criteria, customers identify existing purchasing options, both brands and points of sale. However, to make their final decision, customers only consider a very limited group of alternatives, given that they:

- are not aware of, nor do they have access to, the vast majority of existing insurance options, so that there will always be more insurance options available than customers will ever know of;

- are not aware of the number of known brands, in that there is still a breakdown between the group of evoked brands and the group of inert or inept brands;

- the set of evoked brands refers to the options that customers consider as valid for making a decision. If, however, customers do not have a fixed set of evoked brands, they will search for more information with a view to creating such a set group based on the insurances acknowledged as being indifferent;

- the inert group includes brands to which the customer is indifferent. Despite not making any effort to search for information regarding these options, the customer will accept and process the information regarding the group as available; these may later become acceptable options when there are no evoked brands.

- the inept group covers options that are excluded from any type of consideration because the customer had a bad experience with them, or because they have a poor reputation among the people from whom the customer seeks advice. Even if there is information available on the insurances that fall within the inept group, the customer will not consider or process this information.

In summary, the customer's decision is based on an evaluation of evoked brands, within the assessment criteria relevant to the customer's particular situation. If no satisfactory solution is found, an alternative solution is sought within the inert group, the group of inept options being disregarded whenever possible.

3E5) Market approach and information profile search

The relationship between the choices made by a customer and the presence or absence of a brand in the evoked set, determines the way in which insurers should develop their marketing tactics. There are four possible approaches (as shown in figure 6):

- Maintenance: evoked brand and nominal choice

- Rupture: non-evoked brand is a nominal choice

- Preference: evoked brand and extensive choice Interception: uncalled-for brands and extensive choice

Brand	Nominal Choice	Extended Choice
Evoked	Maintenance	Preference
Non-evoked	Break-away	Interception

Figure 6: Relationship between the type of decision and evoked brands

Maintenance: evoked brand and nominal choice

This is the most favourable situation for insurers since the brand is usually purchased through nominal choice. When a customer needs insurance, choices other than the usual one will not be assessed.

The decisive tactic is based on ensuring that the customer maintains this behaviour, which would require:

- ensuring a friendly and diligent service, good quality of claims settlement and avoiding errors in invoicing processes;

- attributing distribution incentives;

- defending break-away tactics by introducing on-going improvements to insurance and countering promotions and discounts offered by competitors.

Break-away: non-evoked brand and nominal choice

This is the worst case scenario for any insurer in that customers are not customers and do not search for external information, nor do they consider alternative choices, since the brand is not in the evoked set and choices are nominal.

The first challenge is to break the existing decision pattern, which requires developing:

- communication measures specifically designed to break the habit of always making the same choice, in particular through comparative advertising and highlighting the advantages of the insurer and its insurances;

- promotions;

- point of sale advertising;

- distribution channel incentives.

Low involvement learning is important in the medium-term, but is insufficient to change a customer's purchasing patterns in the short-term.

Preference: evoked brand and extensive choice

In this situation, and despite the brand being included in the evoked set, it is still necessary to ensure customer preference, both during and after the process of obtaining information on available insurances. The insurer needs to know where customers get their information and what search criterion is used, so that it can prepare its employees and agents to be able to clear up customer doubts efficiently.

It is also necessary:

- to demonstrate that the insurance performs better than that of its competitors with regard to the attributes decisive to customer choice;

- to prevent attacks from competitors, particularly during times when customers are searching for information in order to make their choice.

- to hear the opinions of current customers, in order to demonstrate the advantages of the insurer and its insurances to potential customers.

- to provide extensive training to the sales force and agents, offering additional incentives when the insurance is recommended;

- to use communication material at sales outlets.

Those having an influence on customers are themselves often the targets of this type of action.

Interception: non-evoked brands and extensive choice

In this situation, customers search for information without considering the insurer brand. The main priorities are to encourage customers to search for information about the brand, to introduce new aspects appreciated by customers and to communicate using campaigns designed for the purpose.

The insurer needs to intercept the customer while searching for information on the evoked brand, making incentives to the distribution channel decisive in positioning the insurer within the customer's range of options.

This approach is also effective in attracting new agents and in increasing the portfolio of agents with which insurers already operate, using trial payments by providing the means for agents to acquire and transfer business as well as monetary awards paid out to those who achieve set objectives.

Public relations and sponsorships are also commonly used to strengthen personal and institutional relations with agents, in particular:

- productivity prizes for agents;
- commercial agreements;
- themed workshops;
- seminars providing different experiences.

3 F) Assessing alternatives and decisions

The customer does not assess the options as a whole. In the decision process, the characteristics of the insurance decisive to the choice are identified and become the assessment criteria. The decision is the result of assessing the performance of available insurance within these criteria.

Decision criteria are the characteristics or attributes that best show the benefits expected by the customer, as well as the costs.

The criteria may be tangible (the premium to be paid, whether or not there is a deductible or the existence of a clinical network in a particular region), or intangible (the attractiveness of a particular advertising campaign or friendly customer care). These can be defined in terms of:

- extremes: insurance with a wider range of coverage, with a lower deductible or that has the most satisfied customers;

- limits, such as a cost of less than $500 or with a liability limit in excess of $5,000,000;

- extent, the case where the excess ranges between 4% and 8%.

Typically, the more complex the products, the more criteria used: it is normal for a lower assessment criterion to be used in purchasing travel insurance, than when purchasing an all risks property insurance.

Customer characteristics, such as education, knowledge, age or social class, also determine the amount of criteria used in making a decision. In purchasing the same type of insurance, one customer may only look at the price while another may wish to compare insurance cover, insured capital limits, deductibles, grace periods and other insurance details.

The circumstances in which a decision is made, such as the time available for making a decision, or the technical competence of an agent, also determine the number of decision criteria used by the customer.

Insurance companies should know the decision criteria used by their customers so as to develop and communicate the qualities of their brands effectively, and also to influence the criteria used by customers, with a view to matching them to their own strengths.

The following facts are important in assessing alternatives:

- many purchases involve little or no assessment of alternatives;

- insurance purchased for emotional reasons involves the anticipation of feelings resulting from the purchase or possession of insurance, instead of an analysis of the nature of the insurance;

- insurance purchased to gain mention at social or other such events, involves the anticipation of third party reactions, rather than an assessment of what the insurance offers.

There are two methods by which to determine the criteria customers use to arrive at any given decision:

- direct, which involves:

  o questioning customers directly on the information used in making a decision;

  o social network comments;

  o specialist article references;

  o insurance comparison studies;

  o observance of references to insurance and what it has to offer in focus groups.

- indirect, on the assumption that customers do not wish, or are unable, to state their assessment criteria, in which case the following examples can be used:

  o projective techniques, in which the customer is asked what criteria other people might use in a certain purchase decision, and more often than not the respondent to the survey provides a personal opinion in responding for others;

- perceptual maps, in which customers compare alternative brands according to their own assessments and the factors they most value, without receiving any assessment criteria beforehand.

After the criteria customers use to make their decision are identified, the relative importance attached to each criterion is ascertained. This factor is important because customers may use the same decision criteria but attach a different degree of importance to them, causing them to make different choices.

The relative importance of each factor varies according to individuals and the case in question. There are direct and indirect methods to determine what degree of importance customers attach to their decision criteria, in particular:

- Constant Sum Scaling is a direct method in which customers allocate 100 points to each assessment criterion, according to the relative importance attached to it;

- Conjoint Analysis is an indirect method in which customers value the different features of an individual product and customer preferences are assessed as and when the values of these attributes vary. This method results in a curve of preferences that reflects the importance of that specific attribute. This method helps identify cases such as a variation in premium being of very little importance if its cost falls, although should its costs rise it becomes more important.

Assessment criteria and the importance attached to them by customers do not just influence selected brands, but also can determine if and when a purchase is made, if and when there is a recognised need to purchase.

Lastly, the assessment made by customers of the options considered for purchase must be determined, for each assessment criterion. Here the extremely simple technique of the scale of semantic differentials can be used. This is based on a scale of performance levels from 'good' to 'bad' for each of the criteria presented, with 5 to 7 ratings between the two extremes. Customers rate the insurance performance according to this scale.

3G) Customer limitations in their ability to assess alternatives

The vast majority of customers are not prepared to assess insurance performance using complex assessment criteria. For simple criteria such as price, customers are more able to judge. Even then, the analysis can be very complex in its indexation to the quality of the product and the way in which it can be affected by other variables.

In conceptual terms, a valid comparison between insurances is very difficult for the ordinary customer because:

- Small differences between alternative brands are not identified.

  The minimum level to which the attributes of a brand differ from one another, in differences the customer can identify, is the "minimum perceptible difference". This concept is of great importance, as insurance is often improved and customers do not value the improvements because they do not notice them. The inclusion of a particular type of cover, such as providing assistance to pets in motor insurance policies, may not increase the perceived value of the product, although it will increase its cost.

- Insurance is an intrinsically complex product, including a set number of clauses covering the general, particular and special conditions of the insurance, which as a general rule, are not read or understood by most customers;

- The performance of certain attributes can only be assessed after extensive use.

  The speed with which claims are settled or whether the amount of compensation is adequate for losses incurred are important decision criteria that can only be assessed after a claim has been made. 80% of customers never make a claim.

Customers unable to assess alternative insurance adequately may make poor purchase options. This is of major concern to regulatory bodies, customer defence associations and also to those responsible for companies offering insurance proposals costing more than those of their competitors.

Customers also recognise their inability to assess and compare certain details of the insurance and this leads them to use replacement indicators. From the performance analysis of an attribute that the customer can assess, an assumption is made on how the insurance performs in other attributes important to the customer, but which the latter is unable to assess.

Customers often use observable attributes as indicators of the performance of non-observable attributes. The observable attribute works as a replacement indicator.

The level to which the customer believes in the replacement indicator, depends on estimated value and confidence value.

- The estimated value is the validity of an attribute to indicate the performance of another attribute. An insurer that has been in business for over a century is often interpreted as being solid and reliable. In this case, seniority is given a high estimated value based on the solidity and confidence of the insurer and consequently of its insurance.

- The confidence value refers to the ease with which customers observe the performance of the replacement indicator. The most used replacement indicator is likely to be price, due to its confidence value.

Replacement indicators are based on the customer assuming that directly associated insurance characteristics exist, such as price and sum insured by a policy, or the relationship of price to deductible, and factors that are not related, such as the diversity of cover and friendly customer care.

The brand image is often used as a quality replacement indicator as it is a highly important factor when it is the only information the customer has available, consequently reducing the importance of the price factor. Other factors also frequently used as quality indicators are the origin of the insurer, the diversity of guarantees, advertising, associated services, brand strength, document presentation and the colours and styles of the materials used by the insurer.

Insurers need to be aware of the existence of this type of customer assumption to avoid counting on factors that customers assume to be mutually exclusive.

Insurers must assess whether the characteristics of their insurance exceed the "minimum perceptible difference" and must know the replacement indicators used by their customers. These two aspects are fundamental to the development of a business plan for products and a communication plan that is effective for target segments.

3H) Application of rules of decision

After identifying evoked brands, to determine the essential criteria for comparing alternatives and assessing performance in the choice criteria, customers apply rules of decision to make their final choice. The main rules of decision are as follows:

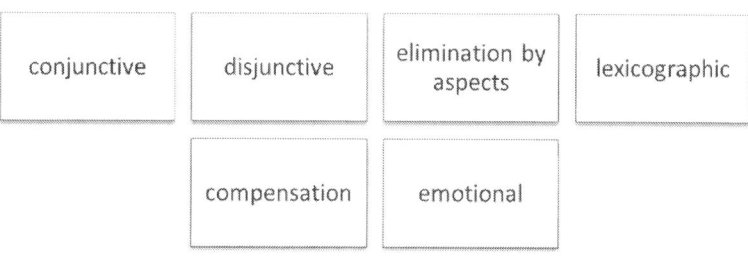

Figure 7: Customer rules of decision

3H1) The conjunctive rule

In this rule all (some, or the first) insurances are selected that exceed the minimum performance levels in all relevant criteria. If several brands are above minimum values, customers tend to rely on other rules of decision in order to make a final choice.

It is a very simple rule that reduces the amount of information processed by customers to levels that are more easily managed, particularly in the more complex decision processes.

3H2) The disjunctive rule

This rule selects all (some, or the first) options that exceed a satisfactory level of performance (usually high), in any of the decision criteria. Similar to the conjunctive rule, the customer can purchase the first brand that is considered acceptable (particularly with low involvement purchases), turning to another rule of decision (in the case of high involvement purchases), or the customer can consider other criteria.

3H3) Rule of elimination by criterion

In this rule, evaluation criteria are arranged in order of importance and the definition of a target value or cut-off point applied. All brands are considered for the most important criteria, and those in which the performance falls below the target value are excluded. If more than one option exceeds that value, the process is repeated using the second most important criterion, and so on, until only one option remains.

3H4) Lexicographic rule

In this rule criteria are arranged in order of importance. The customer then compares insurance performances in the most important criterion and chooses the best. If more than one brand performs equally well in this criterion the process is repeated using the second most important factor, and so on, until only one option remains.

This rule is very similar to the previous one, the difference being that the best performance is sought in each, while in the previous rule only satisfactory performances in each of the criterion are sought.

If this rule is applied it is essential for the insurance to equal or exceed the performance of all competitors in the most important criteria. Good performances in less important criteria are irrelevant if the brand is not strong in the most important ones.

3H5) Rule of compensation

Previous rules are non-compensatory in that the best performances in some criteria do not compensate for poorer performances in others.

This rule is different in that it takes into consideration the performance of each relevant criterion and calculates a weighted score for each insurance. The customer selects the option that scores highest among the alternatives assessed in this way.

3H6) Emotional choice

In this case, brands are not broken down into criterion for individual analysis or assessment. Alternatives are assessed from a perception of how each option makes the customer feel after buying or using it.

3H7) Main elements to be considered in applying the rules of decision

The rules of decision are procedures used by customers to facilitate their choices, and are often applied subconsciously.

Insurers should know the rules used by their target customers and adapt their products, services and communication to the way in which information is gathered and processed. The application of different rules may give rise to different choices. Customer profile, the type of insurance and the circumstances in which the choice is made, influence the type of decision rule applied.

This concept is simplified because it does not detail the importance of the distribution channel (which could be an agent, broker or bank employee), which often accompanies and influences the customer throughout the decision process.

There are a series of aspects important in the application of Customer Decision Rules:

- in low involvement purchases, customers aim to minimise the psychological cost of the decision, using the simpler conjunctive, disjunctive and lexicographic decision rules, as well as elimination by criterion;

- in high involvement or higher risk purchases, customers tend to increase the effort applied in the decision process, adopting more complex and sophisticated rules, such as the rule of compensation;

- the conjunctive and disjunctive decision rules also serve to restrict the number of alternatives in complex decisions when there are many brands in the evoked set by generating a subset of fewer options.

All remaining rules point only to a single customer option.

3I) Neuromarketing

Many new products launched on the market are not successful, despite companies using market research processes and customer analysis to assess their potential interest.

Taking account of the fact that:

- the process of launching new solutions is usually handled with due care;

- companies invest significant amounts in market research to reduce the possibility of failure;

- most insurers use techniques that generate scientifically valid results;

how do we explain the high failure rate in launching, developing and formatting new insurances?

The reason seems to be that customer responses to market surveys are not always a close reflection of the way they behave. In many cases, what customers say is not a good indication of how they will behave.

Most customers make subconscious decisions (experiences, information, memories, associations), while market research is based on thoughts and rational reflection, producing conscious opinions. For customer choice, the human brain gathers and analyses memories, facts and emotions, which generate a response that dictates what to purchase. To understand the true customer choice underlying the customer decision, the customer brain would have to be consulted directly.

If decisions were completely rational, market studies would give accurate and reliable answers, and only insurance with a guaranteed rate of success would be launched. However, reality is much more complex. Market research does not decipher the foundations of customer behaviour in most of its decision-making processes.

Conscious factors only explain customer behaviour in very complex customer cases and in post-purchase assessment.

This limitation to predicting customer behaviour can be overcome by using complementary traditional market research methods such as neuromarketing. This technique consists of deciphering the thoughts, actions and subconscious desires of the customer's subconscious mind that motivate customer choice. Neuromarketing is based on the fact that certain regions of the brain are associated with specific cognitive operations. The customer's subconscious desire can be deciphered by identifying the region of the brain that reacts to each type of stimulus, and the way in which this occurs.

Neuromarketing seems to be the way in which to predict, reliably and scientifically, the failure or success of the insurance. This is the key to a true and complete understanding of the customer's thoughts, feelings, reasons, needs and desires. Direct access to the mind of the customer is necessary to be able to assess customer behaviour.

More and more companies are likely to use this technique, obviously beginning with companies that have the financial capacity for it, given the high cost of implementing it and replacing, if only partially, the investment required for traditional market research. It is also likely that more use of neuromarketing techniques will make it even more accessible and, consequently, more available to insurers.

In making general use of neuromarketing the ethical issues involved should be borne in mind, given their potential for customer manipulation. This technique makes it possible to develop new insurance products, without customers being aware of how they are encouraged to purchase them and, consequently, without activating their rational defences to subconscious customer impulses. However, the better insurers understand the subconscious needs and desires of their customers, the better they will respond to them.

Despite the benefits of neuromarketing, apart from the cost limit to its widespread use there is also the question of how to acquire a representative sample of the customer brain in a given target group. Until this question is resolved there will be no scientific response to this approach.

3J) The particularities of collective customers

The decision-making process in companies is more rational and predictable, but it is also a longer, more complex process to that of private individuals as it involves more people, all with different objectives and responsibilities.

As with the decision-making process of individual customers, the decision-making process in companies involves the following phases:

- identifying the need for consumption;
- search for information;
- assessment and selection of alternatives.

The difference is that in the collective decision-making process there are more entities involved in the different phases and they all introduce their respective priorities and motivations.

The need for an insurance product is not always recognised by the entity that is going to purchase it. The commercial success of insurance companies relies on their ability to recognise the participants at every stage of the decision-making process, as well as the factors that are critical to the choices they make so that proposals can be tailored to their demands.

As with individuals, companies also make nominal, limited and extensive choices, although they tend to make fewer nominal choices.

Companies also have their inept, inert and evoked brands and request proposals only from the evoked brands, although they also consider the inert options. Several entities from different organisational structures within the company are involved in the process of assessing insurance proposals. Each one of these entities values different aspects of the alternatives presented. The insurance proposal most likely to be acquired is the one that is strongest in the most important factors to the more relevant entities of the decision process.

The three factors that determine the type of decision taken in each circumstance are:

- Organisational culture. Some companies are deeply centralised, minimising the delegation of power and responsibilities. In some cases most company purchases must be ratified by upper management, whilst in other cases, following approval of the annual budget, entities within the structure have autonomy in purchase management.

- The importance of the insurance, given that the same type of insurance can take on a different relative importance in companies with different types of businesses. Transport insurance, in the case of a removal company, is so much more important than to a company in a different business sector, which may only occasionally need to make a delivery to a given customer.

- The sum insured. Limitations are often set on the degree of autonomy over expenditure enjoyed by the different hierarchical levels, which means that less expensive insurance may be purchased by departments lower down the hierarchy. However, given the complexity of insurance, there is often an entity in the company specialising in negotiating and contracting insurance and, therefore, responsible for purchasing it.

Usually the decision will be all the more nominal the:

- more decentralised the decision process;
- less important the insurance is to the core business of the company;
- lower the value of the premium.

On the other hand, the decision will be all the more extensive, the:

- greater the culture for concentrating competencies and responsibility in the upper hierarchy;

- more relevant the insurance is to its core business;
- greater the value of the premium.

Lastly, there are two additional aspects of particular importance to the process of companies buying insurance:

- the method and timing of premium payment must comply with the rules set out in the financial plans of the company;
- procedures must be rapid, particularly claim reporting and settlement. Given that claims are more frequent in companies than individuals, this factor is even more important in the decision-making process of the company.

4) Managing the insurance customer

Besides being increasingly different in behaviour, and consequently more difficult to classify, contemporary individual customers are very different from earlier generations of customers (particularly the *baby boomers*[2]) in the way in which they think and behave in the family, society, at work and during leisure time.

Equally radical changes are affecting companies. Regardless of the way they relate to insurance companies, and the means they use to do this, there is always an underlying demand for a customer experience that is fast, easy, simple and low cost.

Within the organisational intelligence of insurance companies, the specific features of each customer must be understood and reflected in solutions and customer relations. Customers choose insurers who respect their idiosyncrasies and who best understand them.

There are three phases to the customer management process: obtaining and organising the information that helps understand the customer, defining the value propositions and adopting the measures to increase its value, as shown in figure 8:

---

[2] Individuals born during the post-World War II period, between 1946 and 1964.

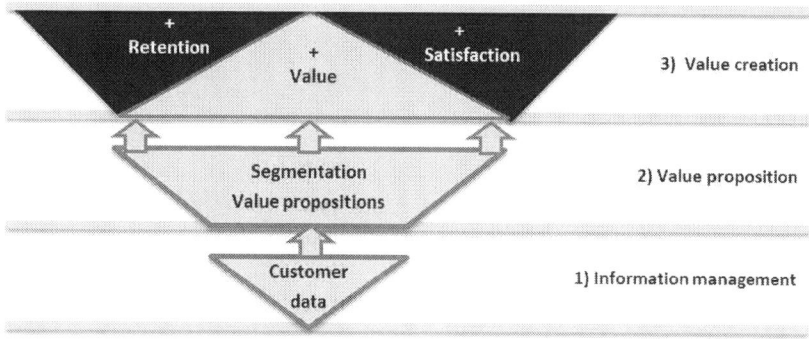

Figure 8: Phases of the customer management process

4A) Customer knowledge

To manage customers strategically means developing a series of organised, strictly controlled, scientifically based activities, which will provide information on who customers are, what their current value is, and the processes required to increase their future value.

To be able to manage their customers, insurers must understand them throughout every stage of their life cycle:

- in the pre-sales process, such as the design of products, advertising them and pricing;

- in the selection and training of employees and distribution channels;

- in identifying potential customers (new or existing, with a cross sales opportunity) and how to approach them;

- in complementary operations such as claims settlement, invoicing and fraud detection.

4A1) Customer value

One of the most important aspects to understanding customers is to identify their current and future value.

The calculation of customer value is based on deducting current and future costs borne by the insurance company in serving customers, from the current and future revenue they will generate. This is a dynamic approach, estimated at the start of a relationship and that must be systematically and periodically re-assessed as further data becomes available from the interaction between the customer and the insurance company.

The assumption in this analysis is that customer behaviour can be standardised, given that customers act according to habit. Consequently their past behaviour can be used to predict their future behaviour. The result of this prediction is the determining factor in defining the type of relationship established with each customer.

The following is a fast and simple way of calculating customer value (CV), and one that can generally be applied to any type of business:

$$CV = \sum_{t'=0}^{T'} \frac{\left[\sum_{i=1}^{N}\left(R'_{it} - C'_{it}\right)\right]}{(1+d)^t} \times P_t - AC$$

Equation 1: Simple calculation of customer value

The meaning of the variables shown is as follows:

- T: dimension of the time horizon considered;
- t: time elapsed since the start of the time horizon considered;
- N: number of insurance policies acquired along the time horizon;
- i: nth insurance acquired;

- R_{it}: insurance revenue i in time t;

- C_{it}: costs directly associated with the insurance i in time t;

- d: cost of capital (or rate of discount) of the insurance company;

- Pt: probability, calculated at the t moment in which the customer remains with the insurance company over the T period;

- AC: cost of customer acquisition, which in simple terms is the cost associated with each interaction with the customer, multiplied by the number of interactions required to attract the customer. These interactions may include, for example, contacts, letters, marketing documents and personal visits.

Two types of adaptation to the insurer business can be introduced into the equation shown:

- The time horizon considered must refer to the expected duration of the customer relationship with the insurance company. Although the duration will vary significantly due to many variables, such as the type of insurance, the common practice is to use a period of 3 to 5 years for non-life or non-financial life insurance, and of 5, 8 or 10 years for financial life insurance;

- Applying the model at constant prices, ignoring the effects of inflation. The error introduced by exclusion of the discount rate or sum insured cost is acceptable, given the scenario of reduced inflation experienced in developed countries over recent years.

Considering the adaptations outlined by the insurance business, the equation has evolved as follows:

$$CV = \sum_{t=0}^{T} \left[\sum_{b=1}^{Nb} Pr_{bt}(CP_b - CO_b) \times CR_b^{(t-1)} + \sum_{f=1}^{Nf} Pr_{ft} \left(CP_f \times RNR_f \times CR_f^{(t-1)} \right) \right] - AC$$

Equation 2: Adapted calculation of customer value

- T: estimated number of years in which the customer will remain with the insurance company;

- b: index identifying each of the non-life[3] insurance and non-financial life insurance products that the customer may acquire;

- N: number of products that the customer may acquire;

- Pr: probability of the customer acquiring the product;

- CP: estimated annual commercial premium of product;

- CO: estimated total annual cost[4] to the insurance company of product;

- CR: estimated rate of customer retention, measured by the likelihood of the customer remaining with the insurance company, in relation to the product;

- f: index that identifies each of the financial life insurance products that the customer may acquire;

- RNR: rate of net return on financial life insurance product f, for the insurance company;

- AC: acquisition cost of each customer.

The equation can be further adapted to the insurance business by excluding non-related claims costs directly from the premium (including the acquisition

---

[3] Comprises general, health and personal insurance, except financial products.

[4] Of these costs, the estimated claims value, the structural costs and commissions paid to agents are of great importance.

cost). Claims costs must remain autonomous because of their importance and specific nature.

If we consider that non-life and non-financial life insurance costs not associated with claims are around 25% of premiums, and that in financial life insurance the average profit level is 0,5% (values that must be adapted to general conditions and to the specific nature of the insurance company), the resulting equation is as follows:

$$CV = \sum_{t=0}^{T} \left[\sum_{b=1}^{Nb} (Pr_{bt} \times 75\% - Cla_{bt}) + \sum_{f=1}^{Nc} Pr_{ft}(Pr_{ft} \times 0,5\%) \right]$$

Equation 3: Insurance customer value with adapted assumptions

- Cla: value of claims on products;

Conclusions on the calculation of customer value

The calculation of customer value is a highly important factor in estimating the current and future results of insurers. Customer value helps the insurance company ascertain the depth and scope of the relationship that it should establish with each customer, distinguishing customers according to the value they generate or deplete. Viewing this as an equation is essential in identifying customers on a scientific basis, demonstrating the most important elements for customer management throughout their life cycle as strategic insurer assets:

- identifying potential customer segments that should be approached;

- ascertaining the level of service and commercial proposals that should be presented to them;

- selecting customers with whom the relationship must be revised or even terminated.

A series of precautions should be adopted in applying customer value to avoid the insurance company adopting the wrong approach:

- poor quality customer data (as outlined in the chapter on customer data);

- failure to identify existing relationships between customers. Customer value may be low when examined independently. However, when customers are related to other customers, either individually or collectively, through family, profession, politics or business ties, they are of direct importance and may be more significant to the insurance company.

- a group of low value customers, when considered as a whole, may represent a very significant volume of business to the insurance company.

These factors do not hinder the calculation of customer value, but they should be monitored and managed in the application of models.

Other considerations in customer management

The calculation of customer value is improved by incorporating variables from traditional segments, such as social and demographic features, which add significantly to the relevance of results.

It is good to know which competitors are aiming to attract the same customers, the way in which they organise and position themselves, the extent to which their objectives coincide, and to be aware of what advantages and disadvantages they have over each segment.

The organizational structure must be flexible and transparent, framed and calibrated by environmental forces that influence the behaviour of all participants.

The process requires a document that summarises the analysis and assessment of data obtained, as well as the approach to be adopted for each customer segment: where to invest and where not invest; how and with which objectives.

The final step involves initiatives based on clearly defined strategic options.

Several indicators are fundamental to customer management. These indicators are underpinned by standard measures within the insurance sector, so that there can be comparability and *benchmarking* between insurers.

Data must be analysed in absolute values and as a percentage variation compared to the same period of the previous year. Apart from basic indicators related to the quantity and value of policies (in force, new and cancelled), and to claims (frequency and average value), some information must be included on *share of wallet*[5] and Net Promoter Score[6]

The following figure shows an example of the summary-table used in approaching each customer segment. Individual sole traders and companies must be dealt with and analysed separately.

---

[5] Dividing the value (or number of policies) of the customer portfolio in the insurance company by the total of its insurance business (or policies)

[6] Difference between the percentage of promoters and detractors. Promoters are respondents that show over 90% interest in recommending the brand; liabilities are customers whose index of recommendation is above 60%, but below 90%; detractors are those that show less than 60% interest in recommending the brand, or in other words, they either do not make any reference or they make a negative comment.

Segment	Main characteristics	Current value Future Value (A)	Priority actions (B)
A	x^1 x^2 x^3	AA	BA
B	y^1 y^2	AB	BB
C	z^1	AC	BC

Current value Future Value (A)	Priority actions (B)
High current value High potential value	Retain and develop
Reduced current value High potential value	Develop
High current value Reduced potential value	Retain
Reduced current value Reduced potential value	Disregard
...	
Potential customers with high value	Conquer

Figure 9: Summary-table for strategic approach to customer segments

All information generated by the Customer Management system, must be inserted into a "Customer Development Plan". There are two parts to this document:

- the first dedicated to strategic issues, with a section dedicated to the assessment of each segment and a final summary chapter on findings and respective guidelines;

- the second, dedicated to tactical and operational issues, outlining the initiatives to be implemented to achieve objectives and an estimate of financial projections and their predicted impact.

Regular reports should be produced containing information on the daily management of the business, namely:

- any gaps between insurance company customer profiles and intended profiles, taking into account all customers, as a whole, and the situation of each segment;

- monitoring customer satisfaction and complaints in each segment;

- summary of environmental and competitive development.

These guidelines are fundamental to strengthening the position of the insurance company in the critical success factors for each of the customer segments. In addition, the following must be ensured:

- a cultural awareness on the part of all employees of the importance of customers to organisational success;

- strict and scientific development of the customer management role;

- technological tools and analytical skills available to maximise the benefits of using the customer information the insurance company has available. Modern customer management is unlike other approaches, concepts and practices that also focus on the importance of the customer in customer business development, such as CRM[7] or Satisfaction Management. Contemporary customer management uses factors developed by these other approaches and integrates them with lessons learnt from other business sciences to create a global model of customer management.

---

[7] An acronym meaning *Customer Relationship Marketing;* this concept emerged in the 1990s, with the development of information technology and communications. The major principal of this concept consists of associating the ability of organisations to establish a personal relationship with each customer with overall business success. For several reasons, many CRM projects did not achieve the expected results, mainly due to over-estimating the importance of technology rather than the unique function (irreplaceable) of employees establishing relationships with customers.

Strategic Customer Management Indicators							
Indicators	Country		Company		Segment (i)		
	Abs	ΔH	Abs	ΔH	Abs	ΔAbs	ΔH	Δ(ΔH)
- # customers							
- Value (€)							
- Share of wallet (€)							
- Share of wallet (# policies)							
- Ø products / customer							
- % customers with non-obligatory products							
- Ø permanency (months)							
- Ø antiquity with the insurer (months)							
- Ø term of payment (days)							
- % policyholders pay by direct debit							
- Satisfaction Index							
- Net Promoter Score							
- % promoters							
- % passives							
- % detractors							
- # policies in force							
- # new policies							
- # canceled policies							
- Ø policies / customer							
- Ø new policies / customer							
- Ø canceled policies / customer							
- € policies in force							
- € new policies							
- € canceled policies							
- Ø € / customer							
- Ø € new policies / customer							
- Ø € canceled policies / customer							
- Ø customer / claims							
- Ø policy / claims							
- Ø € customer / € claims							
- Ø € customer / € policy							

Figure 10: Strategic customer management indicators

Key for figure 10:

- Abs.: absolute value;

- ΔH: percentage variation relative to the same period of the previous year;

- Δ Abs: difference, in absolute value, compared to the same period of the previous year;

- Δ (ΔH): variation, in percentage points, compared to the same period of the previous year;

- Share of wallet ($): dividing the value of the customer portfolio in the insurance company, by its total insurance business;

- Share of wallet (# policies): dividing the number of customer policies provided by that insurer by its total number of insurance policies;

- Net Promoter Score (NPS): method of evaluating the strength of the relationship between the insurer and its customers. The process is based on assessing to what extent the customer recommends the insurer, on a scale of 0 to 10, where 0 is 'never' and 10 is 'recommend fully'. The share of detractors (score between 0 and 6), passives (recommendation is 7 or 8) and promoters (recommendation is 9 or 10) determines the NPS.

4A2) Satisfaction

Customer satisfaction is both a delayed and advanced indicator of the insurer's economic activity: delayed, in that it is the result of what it has done for its customers; advanced, in that it suggests what contribution can be made by its future customers[8].

For many insurance companies satisfaction is paradoxical, given that on the one hand it recognises it is one of the more important indicators in terms of business performance, while, on the other, they do not implement the process

---

[8] Vilares, Coelho, 2005.

to measure it in a systematized way nor the relationship between satisfaction and the insurer's operational results.

It is recognised empirically that the greater the satisfaction in a relationship with the insurance company, the greater the guarantee of that company's development and prosperity, despite no direct connection being established between satisfaction and the quantity and type of insurance purchased by customers, due to the influence of other customer behaviour variables.

The inability to relate the level of customer satisfaction to insurer profits, on a scientific basis, should not prevent or restrict the implementation of satisfaction management programmes, due to clear evidence of the importance of customer satisfaction, as well the satisfaction of all those involved with the insurer's activity, and, consequently, with the insurer's success.

In fact, some insurers are not aware of the level of customer satisfaction, nor of the underlying factors leading to it; others measure customer satisfaction because it is trendy to do so, or because of the need to meet external demands (e.g. quality certification processes). Insurers that belong in any of these categories, tend to evolve to a new level of competitive development that will allow them to:

- recognise the satisfaction level of those to whom they relate;

- identify the factors that determine satisfaction level;

- act on the results obtained by correcting the cause of any dissatisfaction and rewarding good performance.

Insurers that fall into the categories described must overcome this midway point, in which they bear the cost of the process but only enjoy a limited share in the benefits, and move into a new phase in which customer satisfaction is firmly established and becomes central to defining business priorities.

The process of customer satisfaction is multi-faceted, involving various fields of insurance marketing, as suggested in the following figure.

- The starting point of the satisfaction management process is to identify the customers on which the insurance company must focus, according to their value (current and potential);

- Once this sample is selected, the insurance company should gather information on how customers view the company's performance at the main touch points;

- The final phase of the process consists of identifying and implementing measures that improve insurer performance, in those areas that are fundamental to customer satisfaction.

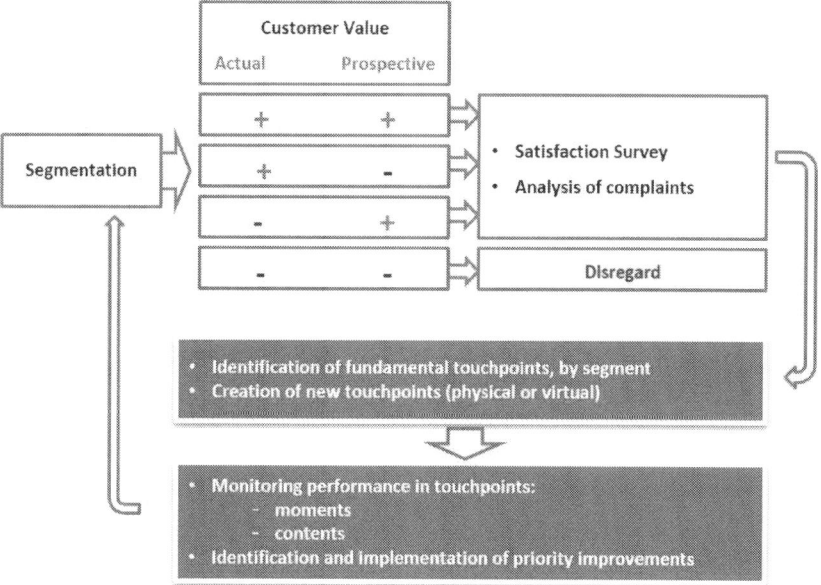

Figure 11: Process of analysing customer satisfaction

A determining factor in the process of customer satisfaction is the use of surveys to get opinions on target subjects. This can be done in two different ways by surveying satisfaction:

- with a specific transaction, such as settlement of a claim;
- with a series of experiences provided by the insurance company.

Although both concepts are used a great deal, the second is a more complete and comprehensive indicator and for that reason relates more to past, present and future performances of the insurance company.

Satisfaction and loyalty

While recognising the importance of customer satisfaction to the economic performance of insurers, the most satisfied customers do not necessarily generate the best results. Satisfaction is determined by what customers feel and say, whereas loyalty is a measure of what customers actually do.

Satisfaction and loyalty are different concepts but both are relevant to insurer management. However they put out different signals and should be dealt with according to their specific nature.

The main difficulties in analysing customer satisfaction are the following:

- Satisfaction is based on regular surveys, or post-event surveys, but these do not reflect any continuity in how customers feel towards the insurance company or what they think of it.

- When a customer is relatively satisfied with an insurance company, the relationship differs depending on whether that same customer has had a good experience in dealing with that insurance company in the past.

- Satisfaction results are often biased. Although statistically this can be controlled, the following issues are not always dealt with adequately and affect the quality of results: cost, time restrictions or the inexperience and incompetence of those involved in the process, problems with non-responses or managing levels of confidence.

Loyalty is also a measure of customer involvement with the insurance company, but one resulting from an analysis of past transactions. The contact and transaction history helps establish the strength of the customer relationship, as well as the way in which that relationship should develop.

Insurers should implement a warning system that, depending on how likely a customer is to assume a certain attitude, triggers the corresponding response, which could be:

- reinforcing, for example, in the case of a cross sale opportunity;

- discouraging, for example, if dealing with a policy cancellation.

However, loyalty is very often based on interest. The customer may relate in no way to the brand but may consider a particular insurance to be more appropriate. The opposite is also seen: although the customer may identify closely with the brand, for external reasons, such as the sale of the insured item, the customer may leave the insurance company.

Satisfaction and loyalty are fundamental indicators in customer management, which complement one another, but do not replace one another. A satisfied customer may not be a loyal customer, while a loyal customer may not be the most satisfied customer. However, despite satisfaction not ensuring loyalty, both concepts are related.

The benefits of measuring satisfaction

Measuring customer satisfaction leads to benefits important to insurers, among them:

- one of the best ways of forecasting the insurers medium to long term success;

- ensuring a focus on the way in which customers are attended;

- providing an immediate understanding of the strengths and weaknesses of the insurance company, as well as market opportunities and threats;

- a major tool in defining business strategy.

However, the following factors may limit the efficacy of the customer satisfaction management process:

- most purchases are nominal, and small scale;

- loyalty is very often polygamous, which means that customers are faithful to a set of evoked brands;

- negative, rather than positive, factors are usually more relevant in the level of customer involvement with the insurance company.

When the results of customer satisfaction measurement do not correspond to insurer expectations, there may be a tendency to disregard the data, bringing about a culture of excuse and blaming bad performance on factors unrelated to insurers, such as environmental, social and cultural issues, or others that are inherent to the actual insurance business. This type of reaction is to be avoided as external factors tend to affect all insurers in the same way, so that the more successful insurance companies are those that manage to offset those adverse environmental factors and, consequently, limit the negative impact on customer satisfaction.

Satisfaction analysis

The process of satisfaction analysis helps:

- understand customer expectations and wishes;

- establish the level to which the insurance company and its main competitors meet those expectations and wishes.

More important than converting negative perceptions into positive impressions, is to actually use satisfaction measurement to prevent negative perceptions from occurring.

Target groups

One of the first definitions in the process of measuring satisfaction is to determine the target groups to be analysed. In addition to existing customers (whether buyers, users, influencers or decision-makers), it is equally important to involve:

- potential customers, who also help identify market opportunities;

- lost customers, who are very important in identifying the insurer's weak points;

- customers of competitor companies, given that they reveal the competitor's strong points, as well as the opportunities and threats to the insurance company itself.

It is equally important to involve non-customers as targets in the process, in particular representatives from distribution channels, due to their influence on the way in which customers perceive their experiences, as well as the major role they play in the customer's purchase decision.

Employees can also become involved in the process, given the importance of their own satisfaction in the quality of the relationship they establish with customers and agents. There are many successful experiences of insurance companies rewarding departments and employees who most contribute towards customer satisfaction. Conducting internal studies in which each employee assesses the degree of satisfaction in services provided by the other departments with which that employee works, are very important indicators in the overall quality of how the insurance company operates.

Critical attributes

The wishes and expectations of customers are confined to a limited set of insurance features, identified as "critical attributes". Customer satisfaction level with the insurance and the insurer is the result of how they perform in these factors. From a customer's perspective, the attributes are perceived in different ways. This perception, which can be expressed statistically, presents relevant variations over time.

The main attributes are as follows:

- basic, which create dissatisfaction when not met, but which do not generate satisfaction when they meet or exceed expectations;

- performance factors that result in satisfaction when they exceed expectations and dissatisfaction when they are not met;

- emotional factors that do not create dissatisfaction when not met, but which do satisfy when they occur.

There are several types of attributes:

- universal;

- specific to the insurance sector;

- characteristics of the actual insurance company.

Other important differences between attributes are:

- image, relative to the insurer's intangible factors;

- transactional, related to tangible characteristics.

Attributes vary depending on:

- the customers analysed;

- the characteristics of the insurance company, such as positioning and objectives;

- environmental circumstances present at a given time.

Analysing customer satisfaction should take into account that not all critical attributes are equally important and results classified according to their relative importance.

From the insurer's internal perspective, employees must be aware of what the critical attributes are when assessing the quality of their own work and in classifying the insurance company.

Satisfaction assessment surveys

Survey design is a determining factor in the success of the satisfaction process. The survey is only as good as the quality of the questions it asks. Structural, generic and standard aspects that must be taken into consideration in designing the survey:

- One part of the survey analyses the public's general satisfaction with the insurance company, and another part relates to individual attributes. These indicators should be compared to levels achieved by the main competitors. Competitors are identified by analysing market shares, employee opinions, in particular those with a commercial role, and by customers themselves when they refer to other insurers from which they also buy insurance. Lastly, surveys must include questions relating to future purchase decisions: the likelihood of re-purchasing and of recommending the insurance company and its insurances to family, friends and acquaintances.

- The order in which questions are placed influences the way in which they are answered. Respondents pay less attention to questions at the end of a survey so it should begin with general questions and then move on to the specific questions. But the ideal solution is to produce different versions of the survey, placing questions randomly in the different versions, to reduce the effect of their position in the survey.

In addition to the questions, other improvements could also be made to the design of surveys, despite raising their cost and response time:

- conclude the survey with an open question that will bring in opinions other than those mentioned in the survey, although the quality of these responses will depend on the ability of respondents to express themselves;

- introduce questions related to individual needs and expectations and allow for identification of specific problems that need to be rectified.

This benefit is very important to some customers who are not bothered about remaining anonymous, and who like this option. However, the insurance company must be able to act quickly to rectify problems detected and, if necessary, solve problems, whilst keeping the customer informed.

Lastly, it is important to be aware of the scale used in the surveys. There are no universal solutions to all cases. The main advantages and disadvantages of the different options are as follows:

- Yes/No scale applies in verifying whether a given event occurred;

- 3-point scale applies to questions dealing specifically with performance, and provide a type of assessment, such as: 'excellent', 'achieved' or 'not achieved';

- a 5, 7 or 10-point scale is often used for measuring attitudes and opinions rather than facts;

- scales of an uneven number are often avoided, on the basis that it is better to remove the neutral point, which serves as a refuge for those who do not have a clear opinion, or who wish to avoid expressing one.

However, not everyone agrees with this approach in that the neutral point is a valuation, just as valid as any other.

- lastly, although more points in a scale provide a more defined opinion, the standard deviation will also vary the more there are, so there is little advantage in using a scale with more than ten points.

Comparison reference

Satisfaction level is usually the result of comparing an initial expectation with perceived performance. The following table shows briefly how target group satisfaction is determined.

	Performance understood in relation to expectation	Better	Equal	Worse
Level of expectation	Below minimum desired performance	Satisfaction	Indifference	Dissatisfaction
	Above minimum desired performance	Satisfaction/ Involvement	Satisfaction	Dissatisfaction

Figure 12: Simplified model for determining satisfaction

This analysis is greatly enhanced if other reference types are used for comparison, namely:

- customer wishes;

- customer experiences when dealing with competitor insurance companies and products;

- assessment when compared to the ideal hypothetical insurer.

Timing and regularity of surveys

Surveys should be conducted as regularly as target groups are contacted. Irregular customer interaction is a feature of the insurance sector, particularly compared to other financial businesses, such as retail banking.

Other factors that could lead to the increased regularity of surveys are changes in insurance company procedures or changes in the competitive environment, which have an impact on services provided to customers.

More regular surveys are recommended when products have just been introduced and when the insurer has more opportunity to react to assess their results.

Furthermore at every important moment in the customer's life, customer satisfaction should be verified, particularly after a claims process.

Application of satisfaction analysis results

The process of satisfaction analysis creates a wealth of information on customers that should be made known throughout the insurance company. The objectives, methods and results of the study should be made known to all employees.

The analysis will be significantly enhanced if the results are compared and consolidated with other types of information. To this effect, the following may be used:

- complaints;
- relative weight of the different segments;
- average customer value;
- growth rate of the different strategic business units;
- results of mystery shopping programmes;
- trends in the main business management indicators;
- internal audits.

The final step is to act resolutely on results obtained. Conducting surveys alone is enough to increase expectations of the insurer's business operation. If expectations are disappointed then resources have been wasted, and the result may lead to those surveyed being dissatisfied.

The following table-grid helps explain priority intervention areas:

		Degree of customer satisfaction	
		Low	High
Importance of attributes (in customer evaluation)	Reduced	Low priority	Unnecessary strengths
	Raised	Attributions to be given the most attention. Priority intervention	Maintenance (insurer strong points)

Figure 13: Priority areas of intervention, based on the customer satisfaction

The customer's expectations must be translated into quantifiable service standards, from which incentives are developed to ensure those performance levels are met.

Making an entity responsible by introducing the necessary improvements, by analysing results and forwarding these to the insurance company's senior management, along with improvement recommendations, is an essential step in ensuring the efficiency of the process.

It is very important for employees to be kept informed of the entire process. The description of jobs and organisational objectives must be closely linked to the results of the study. Systems must be created for acknowledging employees with the best performance levels in meeting the needs of those to whom they relate.

Satisfaction analysis is a never-ending process, insofar as customer expectations and insurer performance are constantly changing. There are no definitive results. Just as most dissatisfied customers do not complain, most satisfied customers do not always volunteer an explanation on why they are satisfied, so they must be asked regularly for their opinions and perceptions.

4A3) Customer experience management

Customer experience management is one of the most important factors in insurer success, but it has not been interpreted clearly and, as a result, its true importance has not received due recognition. Uncertainties regarding the concept are also the result of how it evolved, given that the meaning of experience management today is different to what it was originally.

The initial approach to this concept was to adopt occasional measures in an attempt to change a specific contact into a memorable moment for the customer. This approach became very appealing because it was a way of competing on a platform other than that related to price or insurance coverage.

The current approach is that in all insurer activities and processes, there is either a positive or negative contribution to the customer enjoying a good experience. All operations, people and processes contribute towards providing good customer experiences.

Interactions must be designed according to the customer sector to which they relate. Although all contacts between the customer and the insurer are important from the customer's view of insurer quality, there are some that are particularly important: the moments of truth.

Experience management requires regularly improving the quality perceived in every interaction between the insurer and those it deals with, in a process of creating value for all those involved. The objective is to design interactions that will generate surprisingly positive feelings and emotions, in both community and customer groups, rather than just strictly from the individual point of view.

Current models that explain the customer decision-making process based on cognitive approaches are limited in their ability to explain customer behaviour and must be complemented with emotional models. Recognising the importance of feelings and emotions, together with information on the life cycle of customers, allows the development of customer management models, based on customer experiences.

The best customer experiences are associated with emotional and sensory benefits, although, in the insurance business, there are few measures that seek to make the most of the feelings of customers.

Aromas and sounds may contribute decisively towards customers retaining positive memories of their interactions with insurers, and are particularly recommended in areas where there is underlying tension or where tension is heightened, for example, in places where claims are settled.

The importance of managing customer experiences

Experience management is a good opportunity for distinguishing between insurance companies in an environment where:

- there is ever more choice;

- insurance is more standardised;

- traditional communication is no longer so effective.

This source of distinction is truly powerful, in that it requires no equipment, service or technology, but only the performance of employees and their interactions with customers.

In some cases, satisfied customers may leave their chosen insurer, while dissatisfied customers may not leave the insurer. The fact is that satisfaction studies do not fully reveal the deeper reasons related to customer feelings and emotions. The best customer management model is that which brings the satisfaction study and customer experience management together in a consolidated, integrated process.

The experience concept and its implications for the insurer / customer relationship involves four key[9] moments:

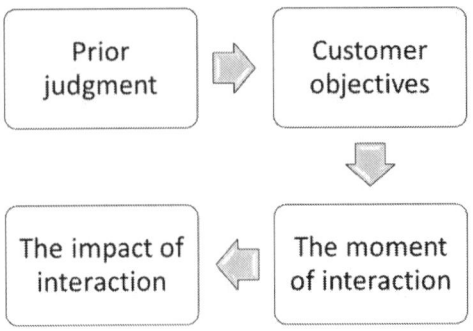

Figure 14 Key moments in customer experience management

Prior judgment

The process of experience management starts long before the actual management begins. The information that each person provides, as well as the individual's personality, affect their interpretation of the experiences offered to them. The implication of these prior judgments on marketing means that insurers need to understand the way in which each segment interprets the experience offered to it, both consciously and subconsciously. If the prior judgment is positive, the non-conformities of the insurance company will be assessed less negatively and the consequences will be less serious than if the prior judgment did not exist. Even when the experience is new, people create a certain expectation from the information they have and from other similar experiences.

This is particularly important to the insurance business, given that society tends to trust it less than other business activities. However, opportunities to change the image society has of insurance are rare because, on average, interaction with the customer is rare, which means that every interaction is highly important.

---

[9]Adapted from Shaw, Dibeehi and Walden(2010)

Managing expectation is a task as important as it is necessary: if the insurance company lowers the expectation level too much to avoid disappointment, it will not attract the customer's preference (the customer opting for a more attractive alternative); but if the insurance company creates an expectation that is too high, it will be easier to attract the customer, although it greatly increases the risk of not rising to that expectation.

Customer objectives

The quality of experience is the result of the extent to which the rational and irrational objectives of the customer are met. This is perceived at the moment of purchase as well as during use. For this reason, selling an insurance that is inexpensive, with low cover, a high excess charge or lower limits to the sum insured, can often be the worst experience when settling claims.

The moment of interaction

Direct interaction with people is always stronger and more emotional than with technologies. For example, an experience in which people intervene can correct errors and clarify doubts. This does not happen when the interaction takes place with a machine.

The impact of interaction

The customer's future choices are largely determined by the way they remember past customer experiences. The experience must trigger feelings in the customer that are memorable. Measureable factors must also be included in experiences, so that customers can rationally justify their emotional decisions. These are insurance characteristics and features that the customer may use to justify choices made, such as the results of satisfaction surveys, service quality indicators, market share value, or even the role the insurer plays in the economy of the region.

The increasing importance of emotional choice models, along with evidence that in many circumstances customers do not express their true opinions in answering traditional satisfaction surveys (for several reasons, but in particular to avoid the consequences of their answers on themselves or others), requires that an emotive and subconscious dimension be included in customer consultation processes.

Neuromarketing is one of the most effective techniques used to measure subconscious impact and emotions in the purchase and use of insurance. However, there are restrictions to its use (as mentioned in chapter 3I). Below is an alternative model for measuring brand-related customer emotion that is simpler, readily accessible and inexpensive, as well as being suitably reliable:

- To identify emotions associated with the creation and reduction of value for an insurance company[10], in particular:

    o value reducers, such as irritation, dissatisfaction, unhappiness, frustration, stress, disappointment or negligence;

    o attention generators, such as interest, stimulation, energising or exploitation;

    o recommendation, related to trust, safety or attention;

    o involvement, related to happiness and a high level of satisfaction,

    the list of emotions, which at every level may vary depending on the business and customer segment under analysis, must be taken into account.

- Instead of questioning customers on emotions, they are asked to select from a list of twenty or thirty options those that most relate to the customer experience and those associated with competitors.

- The customer's true degree of satisfaction, whether rational or irrational, conscious or subconscious, can be determined from the options selected in assessing the experience.

- The insurance company adapts to experiences in order to generate more emotions that will create value and fewer that will reduce value.

---

[10]Adapted from Shaw, Dibeehi and Walden (2010)

Identifying the emotions associated with each interaction is fundamental to experience management.

The process of experience management

There are three determining aspects in customer experience management:

1. identifying the interaction between the customer and the insurance company;

2. defining and designing the way in which the insurance company wants the contact to happen;

3. monitoring the way in which interaction occurs with regard to the initial concept.

The first step in implementing the process of customer experience management is to identify and describe the situations in which occur contacts between the customer and the insurer, in that all interaction between the customer and the company either strengthens or weakens the relationship. The types of contact possible are:

- human vs. technological, e.g. when a customer accesses the insurance company's website or when a phone call is answered by an automated answering system;

- human vs. human, e.g. when providing clarification on a product;

- human vs. environmental, e.g. providing information on a brand, communication campaigns or visits to branch offices.

It may not be possible to exceed customer expectations at all times and in all types of interaction, even with a strong organisational culture committed to this objective, as this would require supervising, measuring and controlling far too many contacts made between insurers and customers. For this reason, the most important interactions with the customer should be identified so that in these particular situations the insurer can guarantee the customer will enjoy an exceptional experience.

The general view is that claims settlements are a decisive moment in the relationship between the customer and the insurer. However, we must remember that most customers do not make claims and, of those that do, a significant number are regarded as bad customers because they generate negative profitability, so this assumption should take these constraints into consideration.

The different customer segments relate to the insurer in different ways, favouring different methods of access. In defining interaction with the insurance company, the preferences of the different segments should be taken into account, the frequency with which they occur and their respective relative importance.

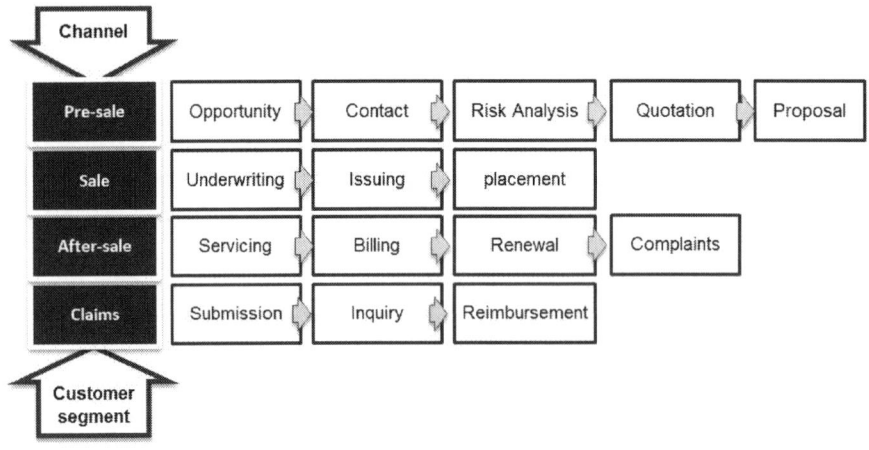

Figure 15 Basic points of contact between insurers and their customers

In addition to the basic points of contact between insurers and their customers (shown in figure 15), other interactions should be considered in order to improve the customer's customer experience.

The second step consists of determining the way in which contacts occur with a view to making them more positive (or even memorable) for the customer, and more efficient for the company. This has to be done consistently and systematically. Competitive advantages can be created by making small changes to the customer interaction process.

The most efficient way to ensure that the customer perceives experiences to be positive, is to involve the actual customer in the design and implementation of those same experiences.

Different types of customer value different types of experience in different ways. Although in the initial stage of the process a basic model of experience can be set up that corresponds to the global intention of customers, the efficiency of the experience management model will have to be adapted to each customer segment as well as to the various distribution channels.

The third step consists of implementing the contact models defined, as well as defining measures that will identify gaps between models designed and events registered. At this stage infrastructure, procedures, policies, technologies and systems are prepared and employees trained ready to act accordingly, ensuring that, once defined, these experiences are provided consistently.

Experiences have to be constantly assessed, controlled and monitored and compared against customer expectations. Improvements should be an on-going concern and an integral part of the organisational culture of the insurance company.

However, experience monitoring should focus primarily on interactions relatively more important to what the customer remembers, and this requires:

- identifying the moments more frequently remembered;
- determining what in the experience is most closely connected to the essentials promised by the brand;

- concentrating efforts and experience management resources on the two situations described above.

The experience of non-priority interactions must be of a quality sufficient to ensure they do not become more relevant due to the dissatisfaction they generate. On the whole, the most important interactions for eliminating any dissatisfaction with the brand are those associated with how the company operates, and with support and assistance. In these areas it is always an advantage to reduce, or where possible eliminate, the visibility of these interactions, given that their contribution towards valuing the brand is potentially negative. Other interactions, of a more ornamental nature, do not contribute to inhibiting or accentuating frustrations that may occur during a customer process, but they are essential in pleasantly surprising customers.

Competitive advantages are developed by designing and providing ornamental interactions in the areas most valued by customers, with a combination of human intervention (which is harder for competitors to copy) and mechanical intervention (in order to be more economically competitive and reliable).

Of the seven most important processes that that have a direct effect on improving interactions, there are those that generate on-going improvement and those more likely to generate disruptive changes.

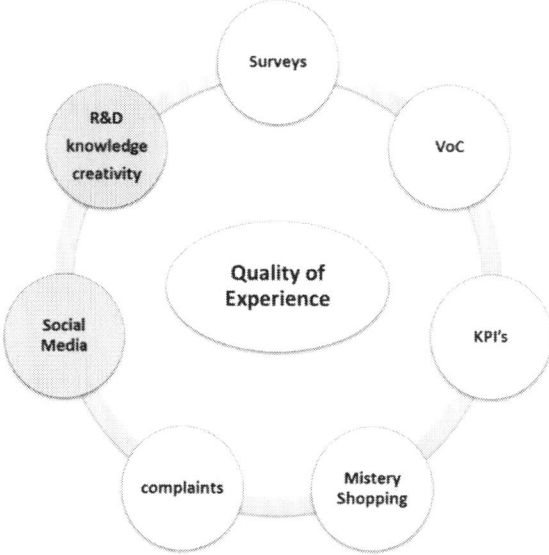

Figure 16: Monitoring the perceived quality of experiences

In the group of processes providing on-going improvement, we have:

- Surveys, such as those handed out to customers after a claims procedure, to check the outcome of their interaction with the insurer.

- "Voice of Customer" programmes that register, analyse and draw conclusions from all customer contact situations with the insurer and others involved with the insurer.

- Key performance indicators that automatically measure the degree to which the different activities are performed. Best practice consists in the insurance company undertaking a commitment to its customers, to respect certain levels of service and, in failing to do so, to compensate customers financially.

- "Mystery shopping" programmes that monitor the way in which the brand is publicised by its main distributors, of particular interest in cases where intermediaries are not exclusive and there is a need to make a comparative assessment of references made to the other insurers represented by that agent.

- Complaints, although, on the whole, there are fewer reasons for customers to complain, they complain all the more, which generates a wealth of information that has to be duly assessed and managed.

The following are processes of much greater impact that can more easily lead to the introduction of disruptive improvements:

- The social media, detailed in chapter 9, where customers report the way in which they assess many of their experiences with insurers.

- All incentives towards innovation and critical thinking, using a wide variety of sources such as solutions found in other industries to resolve problems that are also found in the insurance industry.

4A4) Analytical abilities

The scientific component of marketing is increasingly more important and predominant. The sophistication of marketing tools, new customer demands and the need to be physically or virtually closer to customers and agents, has boosted new methods and tools for understanding customers and for offering them a better deal than that of competitors.

The increasing importance of analytical procedures does not undermine the intuition, instincts and presence of the mind of the manager; it simply means that companies need to know their customers very well, using analytical marketing tools as a way of meeting current competitive demands.

Analytical marketing is distinguished from other competitive intelligence procedures because of its ability to forecast the future, instead of being restricted to reporting past events. Applying statistical techniques to data from entities (usually customers, but could also be other stakeholders) makes the mathematical modelling of behavioural patterns possible. The data needs to be stored and organised into files designed for this purpose.

Many insurance companies find themselves in the following vicious circle that leads to delays in adopting and developing their analytical abilities:

- insurance companies have little, and poor quality, information on their customers;

- the effectiveness of their predictive models is limited, so that large investments are not made in analytical technologies;

- there is an inability to segment and develop value proposals that are truly relevant to customers.

This vicious circle makes it impossible to create value from customer preferences, generating a process of innovation based on an internal understanding of customer behaviour, rather than being based on what customers really desire.

Adding data from customer interactions to information from transactions is a process that has evolved. This information leads to developing skills in applying marketing tactics, risk analysis and improving operational efficiency.

Insurance companies could harness their statistical and actuarial skills far more frequently and intensely to be able to model the purchase behavioural patterns of their customers.

Analytical marketing will continue to change the way in which insurers are managed and decisions are made. Some of the areas where benefits are more evident are[11]:

- in strengthening the insurer's competitive abilities, by developing a source of distinction that cannot be imitated by competitors, achieved using the knowledge acquired in examining its internal data. The insurer may become aware of the specificities of its competitors and respective customers that they themselves are not aware of.

---

[11] Siegel, 2010.

- increasing customer value, by analysing customers, and determining how likely they are to purchase more products or insurance cover, react to marketing stimulus or to leave the insurance company. Based on what the customer is likely to do, the insurer should implement initiatives encouraging customers to adopt behaviour compatible with the company's own interests.

- in strengthening the insurer's protection against fraud. Examining the entire history on fraud will help model circumstances and identify the most likely suspect customers. In these cases the insurer will be prepared for triggering initiatives to prevent their occurrence.

- increasing insurance competitiveness through a better understanding of the risk profiles of each person, each company and each insured item. Supplied with this knowledge, the insurer will be in a better position to be more competitive in good risks and less competitive in bad risks.

- improving the quality of experiences provided to customers, by shaping the insurer's points of contact and communication to customer characteristics and wishes.

This type of analysis can never be completely accurate because of the uncertainties of human behaviour and the occurrence of unforeseeable circumstances in the lives of customers. The implementation of analytical procedures in insurance companies must take into account four types of constraint:

- The inability to predict or even estimate many customer behaviours given the irrationality of some decisions or the influence of variables that are not modelled, such as being in a foul mood or being aware of a bad experience with an insurance policy.

- The importance of integrating the experience and empirical knowledge of employees and insurance company managers in the analysis. These added gains are particularly important because analytical procedures do not have (nor can they have) all relevant information and because mathematical models are not perfect, always lacking the backing of those who know the phenomena and are able to understand, interpret and explain them.

- Not seeking the over-optimisation of procedures, which leads to reducing the speed of decision-making. Situations in which a decision is not made because there is not enough information must be avoided, particularly where there is little information to add value to the quality of the final decision, or when all the information required cannot be obtained.

- Not increasing intolerance to mistakes.

Insurance companies that adopt analytical marketing will undoubtedly be able to manage their customers better and, as a result, increase their value. Insurance companies that use analytical procedures for underwriting, detecting fraud, customer retention or detecting sales opportunities among their agents, are in a much better competitive position than those that do not.

In short, innovation is critical to analytical capacity, which continues to develop and become more sophisticated so as to match growing demands in the competitive insurance sector. However, because analytical capacity is based on data processing and analysis of results, analytical procedures do not stimulate discontinuous innovation. Adopting these procedures should not lead to replacing traditional methods of disruptive innovation, such as designing new solutions, for example the way in which insurance is purchased and used.

Geographic Information System (GIS)

The GIS (geographic information system) is a very useful tool in developing the analytical abilities of the insurer. These technologies associate the information of traditional systems with their geo-referencing, which helps easy and intuitive detection of existing relationships, behaviour patterns and trends, given that they are backed up by images. The GIS is applicable to several areas of marketing, such as:

- identifying the proximity of insured objects and persons to areas where there is a higher risk of claims occurring, adapting safety solutions to these specific characteristics;

- comparing the regional significance of the insurer in relation to its main competitors;

- quantifying and monitoring regional market shares, in highly potential areas that are insufficiently covered by the installed distribution network or, for example, in establishing growth and profitability objectives;

- analysing levels of local awareness or, for example, perceptions associated with the insurer brand;

- determining the relative importance of each line of insurance in each region, as well as in identifying the preferred characteristics of the insurance (in terms of coverage, deductibles or sums insured);

- analysing the geographical coverage of support services to claimants, for example, medical centres or repair workshops and the respective average cost of repairs or treatment;

- determining average premiums, discounts and bonuses practised locally.

Insurance companies already employ these techniques, although in a relatively rudimentary manner, in analysing environmental risks and fraud prevention. However, there is wide room for developing their use in insurer marketing.

4A5) Organisational framework

From the moment the insurer adopts a strategy focused on customer management, it needs to establish a compatible organisational model. The most effective model for the company to increase the value of its customers is based on creating strategic business units focused on servicing major segments, with each of these units responsible for managing the model.

Advantages of models based on customer segments

The organisational model based on customer segments is the one that best aligns the insurer with market requirements. This structure is particularly suited to the insurance industry because:

- the products are complex;

- there is a significant need for advice;

- the reasons for purchasing vary widely;

- customer demands vary.

This model has many advantages over other alternatives, such as operational structures or models that manage types of insurance, because these approaches do not aim primarily at focusing resources on maximising the value of customers, and consequently:

- they do not deal with customers on a consolidated and integrated basis throughout their life-cycle;

- they do not allow for experience management in interactions with the insurer;

- they create more difficulties in solving misunderstandings or in implementing solutions that involve distinct areas of operation.

The structural model centred on the customer is the one that best promotes the conditions for insurers to increase customer value and satisfaction, ensuring greater efficiency in marketing investments, insofar as the insurer specialises in establishing profitable and lasting relationships with its customers.

Main constraints to the structure supported on customer segments

The adoption of structures based on customer segments should be based on a solid organisational development plan that identifies the qualitative and quantitative costs and benefits associated with these changes. The main difficulties that the insurer will come across must be identified, as well as their complexity and the way in which to solve them.

Some constraints to these changes are related to both human and technological resources. The most common are:

- the cultural resistance of employees to change, resulting from a feeling of threat and insecurity, due to reforms made to their work within the organisation;

- the absence of a segmentation model that is sufficiently robust to provide the expertise in the service offered to these customers;

- the lack of detailed and consolidated information on the characteristics, transactions and value of customers;

- the way systems operate in managing products;

- added costs as a result of losses from economies of scale;

- the dissemination of market knowledge throughout the different organisational structures.

All these obstacles can be overcome. Technological changes, although potentially more expensive, are more predictable. Obstacles associated with human resources can be more complex because they are more unpredictable.

In these cases, the best solution is to establish a communication plan that systematically, consistently and reasonably reports on the intended change and keeps employees informed on progress being made in the project.

A series of metrics and indicators should be developed that fulfil the strategic objectives of the insurer and that simultaneously monitor developments. Ideally it should identify the impact of the work of each employee in the achievement of objectives in the departments to which they are assigned, and consequently achieved by the insurer. Performance rewards for those employees who have performed well is particularly effective.

<u>The organisational structure of customer development</u>

An intermediate step in the structuring of the insurer based on customer segments involves implementing a model that:

- unequivocally guides the insurer towards the intended strategy;

- helps overcome the main obstacles in adopting the final model selected.

This intermediate model creates a new department within the insurance company, the "The Customer Development Department", responsible for the following:

- coordinating projects that aim to overcome barriers to developing the organisational model selected;

- promoting a culture of customer care throughout the insurance company. All employees must be aware of the positive and/or negative impact of their activities on the quality of the end service provided to customers;

- implementing projects and initiatives that lead to increased customer value;

- providing the insurer's upper management with information on customer perception, respective development measures and metrics monitoring.

Creating a department with the sole function of managing the way in which the insurer relates to its customers (current and potential), throughout the entire value chain, is a sign, both inside and outside the insurance company, of the importance of customers to that company's strategy and organisation. The impact resulting from this will have a major impact on: employee performance, relationship with business partners and the increase in value created for customers.

The mission of the Customer Development Department is to focus the direction of the entire insurance company on the customer, intervening both internally and externally:

- internally, by determining what should be done differently at all levels (issuance, invoicing, sales, claims, customer service, among others), so that the insurer distinguishes itself in the areas that are most important to customer satisfaction;
- externally, by managing the customer perception of the quality of services provided. This would entail knowing, for example, what deficiencies lead good customers to leave the insurer, and why low-value customers do not purchase more insurance policies or additional cover.

To be truly effective, in terms of hierarchy, this department should come under the control of the chairman or deputy-chairman because of its importance for the success of the insurer, and this would also ensure that the values and principles it develops are made known and implemented in all other departments.

It is essential to provide this employee structure with strong expertise in two core aspects:

- information management, which covers areas such as:

  o marketing information systems, to design and monitor the operation of databases, focused on managing specific groups (data-marts), defining organisational policies and access to information, and to ensure its quality, reliability and regular updating;

  o analytical, in the ability to extract information from data available;

  o competitive intelligence, using processes for the systematic consultation of market trends and moves made by competitors;

- customer service, monitoring and reinventing customer experiences with the insurer;

- commercial stimulation, which besides plenty of imagination, entails creativity and guidance towards results, masters relational aspects so as to create empathy between colleagues, customers, distributors and other entities involved with the insurer.

The investment required to create such a department is large but is quickly compensated with the production of results of considerable strategic importance, such as:

- not subjecting customer management to difficulties in having to deal with several departments, all of which have other priorities and constraints, inevitable in departments with other responsibilities, abilities and vocations;

- arranging the process of customer management as a cycle, controlled and managed in all its phases, from data collection to campaigns for customer recovery (win back);

- providing upper management with indicators and reports on customer value, critical aspects of service and priority measures, with a view to increasing the value of these customers;

- throughout the company, encouraging focus on the customer as a relevant factor to be included in all global and sector-based programmes and projects, already underway or under development;

- providing information to commercial networks that will guide their activities to current or potential higher value segments;

- introducing the philosophy of the "global customer", with a range of financial needs, developing cross-sales with other business areas where there are synergies, which can involve establishing commercial agreements with other companies within the same financial group, or retailers from other business sectors.

Two other important functions alone justify the presence of this department:

- the first, to provide a catalyst for the modernisation and competitiveness of the insurance company, particularly technical, commercial and administrative operations.

- the second, the need to implement tools to monitor how its strategic activity is developing, using competitive performance barometers for this purpose.

The problem of vertical inflexibility

Situations in which the productivity of employees is limited or obstructed by an inflexible, vertical, hierarchical structure, based on a rigid hierarchy of relations between people, must be avoided

Insurance companies employ increasing numbers of employees with considerable relational skills and solid academic and business training. If the organisational model creates barriers to contacts and professional relationships between employees, important benefits that are a result of knowledge exchanges between people with common interests and concerns, are lost.

Horizontal and vertical knowledge exchange is essential to organisational success. Mechanisms must be created in order to encourage interaction between employees that have the same professional interests, even if they do not know each other or do not usually relate. Any employee with information that is relevant to another department must be able to deliver the information to its destination, without being confronted by formal, inhibiting barriers.

In many situations, the restrictions of rigid vertical models are removed by creating matrix structures or *task forces*. However, these solutions can contribute to hindering operations. The difficulty of defining the scope of intervention for each department wastes time and resources on resolving bureaucratic and administrative issues, of no value to the insurer. Sometimes this type of approach leads to undesirable situations in which the same employee has to report to more than one person in charge.

These issues are not resolved by simply flattening the structure, given that its origins are often embedded in cultural behaviour patterns with strong historical roots. It is more important to clarify the relationships and responsibilities of the different departments, encouraging contact network development where knowledge and experiences can be shared on common topics. Another valuable aid is to use the company's web network.

The problem of vertical rigidity can be resolved, basically, by changing attitudes and behaviour and by adopting new information and communication technologies, such as relationship facilitators.

4B) Development of the customer base

In many insurance companies cultural orientation continues to be geared predominantly to product management rather than customer management, making it fairly simple to identify product profitability but very difficult to recognise customer value, as well as the underlying factors. In many cases marketing is not focused on customers and there are no action plans for the different segment types, meaning that good and bad customers are dealt with in exactly the same way (no distinction), at all levels (invoicing, issuance, customer service, among others).

At the same time, the environment in which business is conducted is much more complex. The demand for very short-term results is ever greater, in an environment where radical changes are being made to customer approach, products, communication means and distribution channels.

There are new customer segments. As discussed in the "segmentation" chapter, the traditional concept of family has been changing and varying. Single parent families have been increasing as marketing targets. The difference between the social roles of men and women has narrowed. Gender, which traditionally was one of the main variables in customer segmentation, is far less of a difference. New cultural behaviour patterns have arisen as a result of new migratory flows.

Means of communication have been multiplying and specialising. There are new distribution channels, fragmenting the efforts made by the commercial structures of insurers. Conflict between channels is of constant concern in designing marketing policies.

On the other hand, a succession of management techniques has been implemented, based on cost reduction, quality systems or the re-engineering of processes, which although important in improving short-term business performance, do not ensure the conditions for medium-term sustainability.

To succeed in this environment, effective strategic customer management is vital, but it demands adopting a new paradigm, a new culture and a new value system.

Innovative processes that focus on strengthening the customer relationship and that demand customer participation and involvement must be promoted.

It is the customers in appreciating, or not, the resulting innovation, who create the value they will benefit from, and consequently benefit the insurer.

Customers are no more important now than they were in the past. Customers have always been fundamental to the success of any business. What has changed is the need for them to be adequately managed, using the ever more sophisticated means and tools available.

Customers are the insurer's most important and scarcest asset and must therefore be managed in a scientific, integrated, careful way, which requires:

- systematic customer management using a process within the framework of which inter-related activities can be adequately monitored;

- developing a competitive, global corporate culture, based on knowledge and learning values;

- paying particular attention to detail, ensuring that in each customer contact, regardless of how this interaction takes place, the customer enjoys a positive experience, in this way reinforcing engagement with the brand;

- encouraging employees to be constantly concerned with identifying new ways in which to enhance the customer experience;

- harnessing efficiencies generated in the application of new technologies to customer management. It is essential to master current customer management concepts and technologies and to foresee their future development so as to prepare the insurer for future progress;

- mastering the scientific aspects of strategic customer management. Marketing is a science that has evolved and that must be managed like other organisational operations, namely by applying measurement and control mechanisms. Anything that cannot be measured, cannot be controlled and, consequently, will not be managed;

- adequately managing the time and resources applied to customer management. The prioritisation of short-term activities, with long-term strategic reflection becoming secondary, is an indication of the inefficiency of insurer marketing.

4B1) Testing the experience

In certain types of business, particularly the production of industrial goods, such as the motor trade, testing is one of the main sources of information obtained by customers and used in making their customer choices. There is no reason why service companies that adopt customer experience management programmes cannot use this type of marketing technique. This is the case with the insurance business, where there is tremendous potential for applying the technique, given that the service that gives substance to the contract, which is the settlement of a claim, is provided at a later and unspecified date.

The perception of uncertainty and risk associated with the insurance purchase could be significantly reduced if the potential buyer were to test the service before buying.

Testing can be implemented at an early stage by inviting the customer to simulate the occurrence of a claim and contacting the insurer's claims department. If at this early stage of testing, a fast, efficient and helpful answer is given, and if, besides this, technical ability and professionalism are demonstrated in solving the problem, there will be considerable more certainty in choosing to purchase insurance from this insurance company.

Applying this technique to the insurance sector may be useful in attracting new customers and reinforcing the perception of existing customers that they have made the right choice, which may lead them to buying more insurance or other more complete versions of the same insurance.

4B2) Customer Retention

The relationship between customer loyalty and profitability has been scientifically demonstrated. Insurers that manage to retain customers longer than their competitors will sell more products at higher margins. This is an area where knowledge of the current and future customer value is crucial in:

- selecting customers whose retention is worth investing in;

- quantifying the investments that the insurer will incur in increasing customer retention through additional services, incentives, discounts or other types of benefit associated with permanence that will maximise their value.

As shown in figure 17, a systematic approach to the customer retention process, involves the following phases:

- determining whether the reason for cancelling the contract was:

    o At the initiative of the intermediary as a result of:

    - the need to retain the customer, keeping them on the customer database but transferring them to another insurer, with a view to improving contract conditions. In this case, in order to keep the customer, the insurer must present a better offer and/or reduce the insurance policy premium;

    - reasons arising from the actual agent, with a view to increasing agent remuneration or strengthening its relationship with another insurer. To retain its customer in this situation, the insurer needs to renegotiate the terms of the agent's remuneration or to correct any misunderstanding in its relationship with the agent;

    - the agent is transferring its business to a competitor insurer. In this case the agent's reason for doing this must be determined and an assessment made of whether the initiative can be suspended or even reversed.

- At the initiative of the customer, due to finding a better insurance alternative to the one currently held, or a misunderstanding in the customer's relationship with the insurer. Depending on the current and potential customer value, the insurer must decide on what measures are required to recover the customer by examining the offer, the premium or the relationship.

- At the initiative of the customer, resulting from elimination of the risk. In this case, the insurer should determine whether there is an insured object to replace the one that has ceased to exist and, in this case, approach the customer with a view to proposing a new contract.

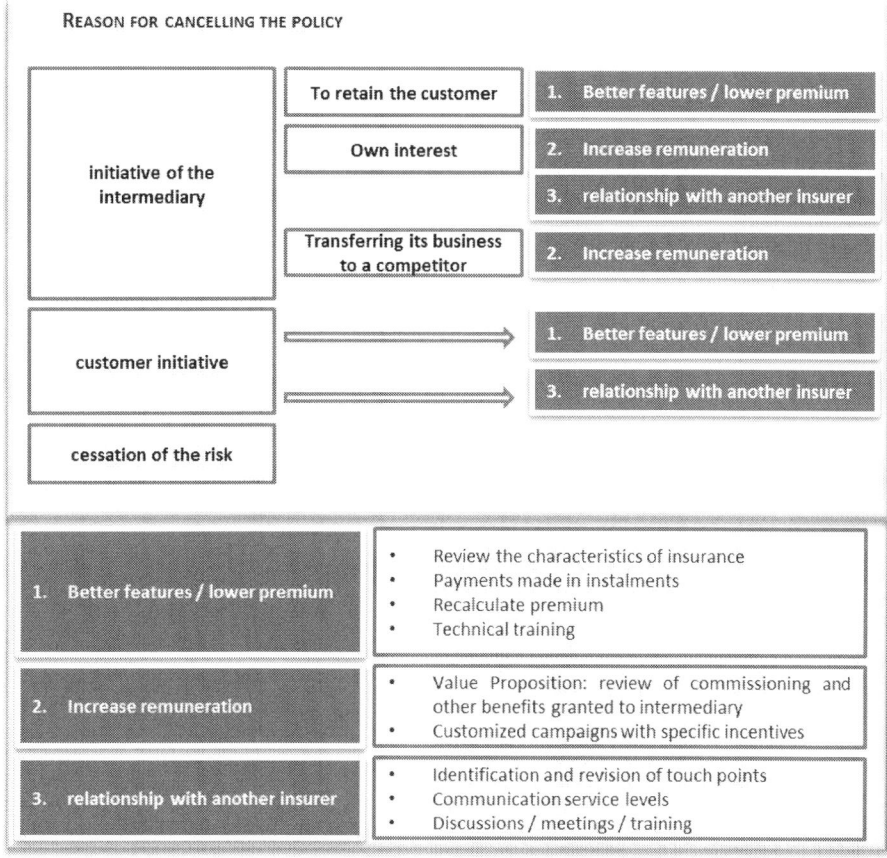

Figure 17: The process of customer retention

Developing analytical skills helps develop mathematical models that determine the probability of each customer leaving the insurer and the underlying reasons for this. Having this type of information available, and overcoming the reasons for leaving the insurer, are highly relevant factors in the success of customer management.

To bring back loyalty, a process that unequivocally identifies the qualitative and quantitative impact of each initiative is essential. This exercise is as necessary as it is complex, given the difficulty in isolating the effect of a certain stimulus from other direct and indirect insurer interactions with the customer, as well as other environmental constraints that also affect customer behaviour.

The effectiveness of this process requires the pre-selection of two random samples of customer:

- a group that represents those subject to the retention initiative;

- a second group with characteristics as close as possible to the first group, but with the difference that they are not encouraged to keep their contracts in force.

The impact of the initiative is determined by comparing the behaviour of the customers in the two groups. This system is used to quantify and qualify the return on the investment made.

Loyalty programmes are fundamental for the insurer to retain its best customers. However, initiatives that generate a positive return must be distinguished from those that do not, and the reasons underlying results determined. Impact monitoring is often underestimated although it is essential for implementing successful programmes.

4B3) Increasing customer value

Increasing customer value is shown in figure 18.

This process must be supported on segmentation that determines current and future customer value:

- if the current customer value is high for the insurer, the priority must be to retain the customer, ensuring that this value is not lost or transferred to another insurer;

- if customers have a high potential value, tactical tools are required that will transfer such value to the insurer;

- if customers have no current or potential value for the insurer, the latter should not invest in developing them as they will bring no returns.

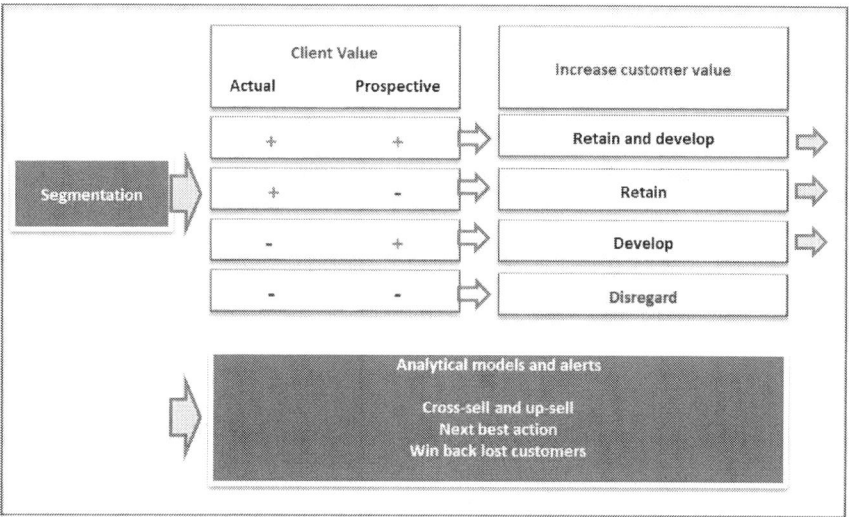

Figure 18: The process of increasing customer value

Cross-selling

Identifying customer needs is the first step to increasing their value.

The gap between the products that a customer already has, and that resulting from the customer's social, demographic, psychological and life style characteristics, must be analysed. Identifying these needs may begin by checking the feelings and opinions of internal employees and agents, and should be complemented by analysis and direct enquiries made to customers.

Besides active customer needs, there are other needs that are inactive because the customer is unaware of their existence. Insurers should make their customers aware of insurance alternatives and the existence of new needs. A study into the emotions associated with the use of insurance is very important and aims to improve user experience and eliminate any factors that cause discomfort and concern to policy holders.

In the initial approach to a customer, it is advisable to use systems that can shape the best insurance solutions based on:

- customer characteristics and needs;

- quotes that can be applied in transferring personal and property risks to an insurance company.

In dealing with existing customers, opportunities to increase their value can include comparing their existing insurance policies with the entire universe of safety solutions that respond to their active and inactive needs. Any mismatches correspond to unmet needs and become a sales opportunity for the insurer.

Moreover, opportunities to increase customer value may also include replacing the customer's incomplete or out-dated insurance cover by something more suited to the customer profile.

Next Best Action

Identifying the "next best action" to be made is now covered by analytical marketing, a successful tool due to the benefits it generates for customers, intermediaries and the insurer itself:

- customers are offered the insurance and the information they need, even if they are not aware of its importance;

- it enables intermediaries to offer valued advice to customers, in this way serving them better and increasing their value, and as a result increasing their own income;

- the insurer serves its customers and partners better by harnessing business opportunities that would otherwise have been lost, while at the same time increasing the productivity of the distribution network and customer value.

The main restrictions to using this method are that it is impossible to identify customer life circumstances that determine insurance needs and, in the event of distributors not being exclusive, they could propose a solution that the customer already has, but with another insurer with which the distributor also works.

Campaigns

There are fundamental measures that insurers can adopt to increase customer value. These involve identifying discrepancies between the products that customers might have and those that they actually have. These are simple and unsophisticated models that can serve as an important first step in the process of customer management.

The next step is carried out when insurers acquire *data-mining* technologies and develop statistics and mathematical skills that allow them to address predictive marketing. At this stage, customer value can be significantly increased by carrying out cross-sales campaigns and by improving product level for current customers, based on analytical models that indicate which customers are more likely to acquire a given insurance and which is their "next best offer". This information helps build proposals that are more suitable to the customer profile, and can be used when customers need them. All customer interactions with the insurer are opportunities to raise customer awareness of the need to increase their level of protection and safety:

- those that occur at the initiative of the customer, such as when they go to a help desk;

- those that occur at the initiative of the insurer, such as when customers are contacted to purchase a certain insurance.

However, for these models to be effective, the insurer must have complete and reliable data on its customers and be able to segment them, matching their value with other transactional and socio-demographic characteristics. Otherwise, no matter how sophisticated the support technology and the analytical skills of the organisation, these campaigns will not be effective, thwarting the expectations of participants and discrediting initiatives and the people involved in such projects.

4B4) Mobility

Mobility is an insurmountable reality these days. Mobile connections continue to register very high annual growth rates, particularly in developing countries. Forecasts indicate that more than half the world's population already has mobile devices. The overwhelming majority of world brands already use mobile communications to interact with their customers.

This group of indicators is the result of the association of two unique mobility characteristics: customisation and availability.

This is a medium that works by itself, by providing information and alerts directed at customers. But mobility is particularly effective when complemented by other communication channels, such as Internet websites, call centres or sales networks, through multi-channel projects.

This channel also opens up unprecedented opportunities for remote working, providing instant access to data, marketing and financial information and others, required in the work of the insurer's employees, as well as for remote access by others with whom the insurer is in contact (customers, suppliers, authorities, distributors, etc.).

The fundamental challenge to the success of this business channel is to ensure that customers value these interactions. The customer's ability to assimilate information is limited. The customer tailored approach used by this channel means that any contact not responding to the customer's current needs is regarded as intrusive. Insurance companies that make contact with their current or potential customers using messages unrelated to their interests, will be permanently deleted from the golden list of those to whom it is worth paying attention.

Competitive benefits of mobility

Mobility is significantly changing insurance business models. The time resource is increasingly scarce and, consequently, more valued. Mobility allows customers to gain access to information and solutions in order to manage their risks, at any time, regardless of their circumstances.

Technologies allow policyholders to conduct their interactions with the insurer (insurance claims, premium simulation, consultations and payments, among others), regardless of where they are, by using their mobile devices. Business partners as well, particularly agents, demand remote access for applications that help them manage the business, with maximum speed and simplicity at minimum cost. Insurance companies themselves can no longer do without the value brought in by remote access to their systems and applications.

The proliferation of communication equipment and mobile information helps determine the exact location of each individual and to communicate with relevant content. Insurers can tell customers which branch or medical centre is nearest to them, suggesting the quickest way to get there and ensuring they receive immediate attention.

In short, mobility brings inevitable benefits to the quality of customer relationships, respecting the following requirements:

- constant and immediate availability of the insurer to attend to customers. Customers do not know when they will require an insurer, or if they will ever need one. However, they want to be sure that if the need arises, the insurer will react quickly and efficiently;

- avoiding a lack of information that may lead to lost opportunities in creating positive experiences for those in contact with, or doing business with, the insurer;

- controlling at an early stage any misunderstanding and its impact on customer experiences, and preventing it from escalating or becoming more serious.

The impact of mobility on the insurer's business model must be predicted, and a response found to matters such as:

- the compatibility of mobility programmes with the overall system of strategic customer management;

- priority intervention areas;

- the skills and resources required to implement mobility projects;

- ethical, legal and statutory issues that arise, such as those related to the privacy of personal data;

- determining moments and circumstances at which initiatives must be triggered.

Circumstances that create difficulties or limit the insurer's ability to enter the world of mobility decisively must be taken into account, such as:

- technological problems due to the diversity of existing platforms that can give rise to difficulties in integrating the different systems and making them compatible;

- transaction security issues that will tend to increase as information itself increases and flows through mobility support infrastructures.

5) Marketing Plan

The marketing plan plays a fundamental role for insurers in:

- formalising business strategy and tactics, as well as their implementation and control, ensuring that there is no doubt as to their meaning;

- developing the underlying process. Insurance company managers should take time to reflect on the following:

    o analysis of the external environment, identifying the main opportunities and threats, characterising the main demographic, social, cultural, economic, ethical, legal and regulatory trends.

    o assessment of major internal strengths and weaknesses, which may be congenital or circumstantial, as well as the way in which they should be reduced or accentuated.

    This reflection is essential in raising an awareness of the factors that led the insurance company into its current situation and what should be changed to increase its success.

    o quantifying what it wishes to achieve, by defining goals and objectives associated with business development, using aggregated and segmented forecasts for the insurance sector, on the market, the insurer and the main competitors, namely:

        - the turnover of new, continued and cancelled insurance policies;

        - policy development

        - rates and frequency of claims;

        - average premiums.

Distribution channels, commercial and regional offices, branches or delegations, technical and commercial agents should all make use of these indicators.

Goals, objectives, projects and priorities should be disseminated and shared by company employees, mobilising them all around the same vision and recognising the importance of their contribution to collective success.

o The definition of Insurer strategy and implementation of the same by planning business tactics together with the teams involved, and duly scheduling the process;

o The establishment of monitoring, follow-up and control procedures, for executing tactical business plans and the achievement level of goals and objectives.

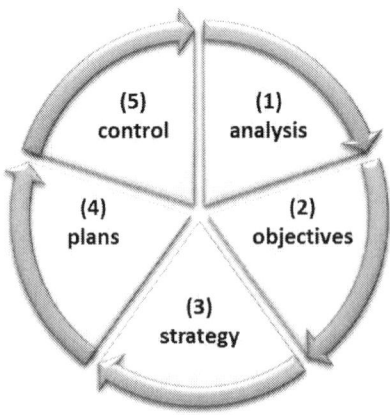

Figure 19: Process of marketing planning

5A) Business strategy and tactics

Defining strategy is one component of the insurer's marketing plan.

Strategy is a concept of business management, the meaning of which is sometimes fuzzy. There are several definitions of strategy, emphasising different aspects to which each author is more sensitive as a result of that author's own personal and professional experiences.

The following definitions should be considered in establishing a unique concept of "business strategy":

- what a company can do as a result of its strong and weak points, and the extent to which it can act depending on opportunities and environmental threats (Kenneth Andrews);

- the way that the company positions itself and the bases for its competitive strengths (Michael Porter);

- preparing an action plan that develops, systematises and applies the competitive advantages of the company (Bruce Henderson);

- a plan that aims to provide the company with a competitive advantage over its competitors, based on distinction (David Collins).

The most common concepts of strategy fall within the following schools:

- Positioning, according to which the strategy aims to create and maintain a relevant and distinct competitive advantage. This model was based initially on military strategy, namely the doctrines of Sun Tzu, Carl Von Clausewitz and Napoleon and had as its main exponents, Bruce Henderson, Kenneth Andrews, Igor Ansoff, Michael Porter and Chan Kin with Renee Mauborgne.

- Execution, claiming that strategy consists of constantly seeking operational excellence, resulting from the introduction of regular improvements to processes and technologies, as well as in alignment with people. This belief was driven initially by Abernathy with Hays, and was significantly developed by Deming, Hammer with Champy and, more recently, by Charan with Bossidy.

- Adaptation, considering that strategy consists of constantly seeking new solutions, based on testing and openness to change and innovation. According to this belief, the main characteristics of excellent companies lie in their ability to act quickly and in the creativity of their human resources. The main exponents of this belief are Tom Peters and Henry Mintzberg.

- Concentrating on fundamental competences, which stipulates that strategy is based on creating value based on the company's core business. The main authors associated with this concept are Hammel, Prahalad and Zook.

All these perspectives make relevant contributions to the correct concept of strategy. However, for the sake of simplicity and respect for the original bases of the concept, we have adopted the definition of strategy as being "where" the company wants to be and "where" it does not want to be[12].

In business terms, the strategic "where" refers to:

- geographical location, bearing in mind:
    - the physical presence of the insurer, its representatives and distributors;
    - virtual presence, relating to places where the insurer does business via the web ;

---

[12] Vasconcellos and Sá, 1996.

Both dimensions are important because in providing services in a given region, the insurer needs to comply with legal, regulatory and operational requirements.

- business or activity;

- customer segments.

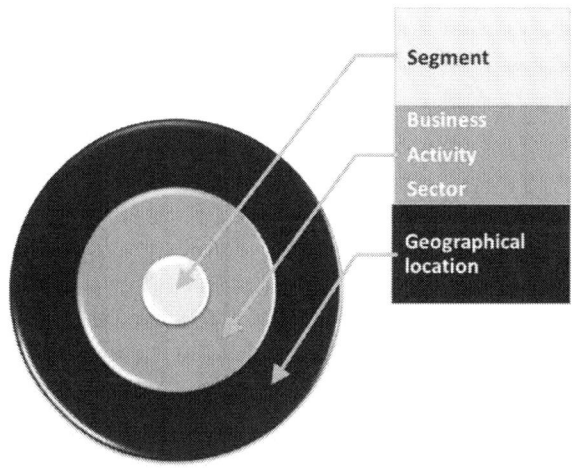

Figure 20: Defining the strategic "where"

This is a simple and objective meaning to strategy concept that respects its military origins. By exclusion, this approach identifies the tactics as "how" the insurer stands in each of the strategically selected segments, in other words, the operations of its corporate structure.

Strategy should not be associated with what is more important, unlike tactics, which deal with what is less important. All decisions can be very important or only slightly important, regardless of whether they are tactical or strategic. Even operational issues can generate serious problems or major benefits for the insurer. In the insurance business, an incorrect operational decision, i.e., underwriting a bad risk, can give rise to serious economic and financial problems.

Long-term decisions should not be associated with strategy either, in that they could become decisions that radically change the direction of the company, with immediate impact. Similarly, an operational decision to implement a basic procedure can remain in force for several years.

The example of the Battle of the Bulge illustrates these business strategy concepts.

The Battle of the Bulge

At the end of 1944, Germany was facing a very difficult situation, defending itself against the Allies, attacking on the western front, and Soviet forces that were preparing to launch a large-scale attack on the eastern front.

After taking Normandy at the end of July 1944, the Allies, disembarking in Southern France on 15th August 1944, advanced with stolid determination towards Germany. To the east, Stalin's forces had inflicted serious losses on the German troops, in an operation where progress had been suspended due to difficulties in supplies reaching the excessively long front line.

Given the fast dwindling supplies reaching Hitler's troops, it was impossible to defend the two fronts at the same time. The only solution was to neutralise the allied forces, on the one hand to be able to concentrate the German forces on defending against the foreseeable Soviet attack, and on the other, to gain some extra time to develop and produce new weaponry.

The Germans believed that the probabilities of a victory would be greater in attacking the allied forces rather than the Soviets, due, among other reasons, to a smaller number of allied troops. Nonetheless, and although considering this battle to be indispensable, given that the defensive strategy adopted in Normandy since D-day (6 June) would only postpone defeat, the Nazi field marshal Walther Model estimated the probability of Germany success in a battle against the allies to be less than ten per cent.

On 11th and 12th December, Hitler organised a meeting with the leading commanders on the western front, in his Eagle's Nest, in Bavaria, where he asserted that a victory over the allies was the last chance to change the course of the war, so that the only possible alternatives were to advance or die.

The plan was to recapture Antwerp, which had been one of the main supply ports for the allies since 26th November, the aim being to divide and defeat the allies so that they would be forced to negotiate peace treaties with the Axis nations.

The Battle of the Bulge (also known as *the Battle of Arden*), took place between 16th December 1944 and 25th January 1945, in what would become Germany's final great counter-offensive in the west, crossing the forest of Arden, in Walloon (Belgium).

The strategy

The first German decision consisted of defining the strategy, determining where the attack would occur. The three alternatives were as follows:

- to develop a major manoeuvre to encircle the US forces in Aachen, isolating the 9th and 3rd armies;

- to attack the least defended areas in Arden, dividing the American and British armies and capturing Antwerp;

- to attack the allied forces in the eastern part of Belgium and Luxembourg, but after Arden, instead of advancing west/north-west, moving north to avoid crossing the Meuse River.

In all three cases, the first target was the American forces, because Hitler wanted to exploit the heavy impact a massive loss of men in a European battle would have on American public opinion.

The strategic decision fell on the second option, repeating the movement that was successful in 1940, given that:

- the siege would be ineffective, due to the weakness of the German forces;

- it was essential to exploit division among the allied forces, particularly rivalries between Montgomery and Patton. Taking Antwerp would isolate the four armies of the allied forces and, in this way, force them to reassess their plans to move into European territory, given that American and British interests did not coincide;

- the third alternative was a less ambitious one and far too slow, bearing in mind the need to move German troops at a later date for the defence against the Russian offensive.

The tactics

The tactics depend on strategy, so after determining the strategic "where", the German forces defined the tactical "how".

Hitler again adopted a military tactic that had been a great success at the start of the war: the *blitzkrieg*. This tactic was based on a fast and decisive surprise attack, with the aim of upsetting and demoralising enemy defence lines.

Given the great airborne advantage of the allied forces, poor weather conditions became a decisive factor in the German decision to launch the offensive.

The 6th Panzer Division of the SS logged the first attack, coming in from the northwest, with the aim of reaching Liège. Among other fairly incredible actions, the German soldiers disguised themselves as allied soldiers, and after crossing the American line changed the road signs to cause confusion and in this way gain time and strategic positions.

The 5th Panzer Army was instructed to capture Brussels, attacking the cities of Bastogne and St. Vith, where major roads intersected.

The 7th Army advanced on Luxembourg to protect the southern flank from Patton's armies, while the 15th Army, located to the north of Arden, was to destroy the American garrisons in the region of Aachen.

Critical success factors

The German forces had a very relevant combination of vulnerabilities, such as:

- air force limitations, further weakened by the fight against the Russians, particularly the violent battle of Kursk;

- low morale, with obvious signs of fatigue and lack of motivation;

- the absence of troops in infantry units as a result of having to maintain the Eastern front adequately garrisoned. This meant that very young fighters had to be deployed and they were poorly prepared for war, both physically and psychologically, as well as ex-combatants who were on reserve;

- the lack of supply of basic materials for the war effort, such as petrol. After the bombing of Romanian refineries, their supply was seriously restricted.

On the other hand, in their favour they had:

- the surprise factor;

- allies with supply difficulties;

- the length of the enemy attack lines, which stretched from Southern France to Holland.

So the success of this battle, which was highly unlikely as the Germans themselves were aware, would depend on performance in the following areas:

- the speed and accuracy of attack, given the importance of the surprise factor so as to take advantage of the enemy's weaknesses. The allied troops were not expecting a German attack, coming mainly from the forest of Arden;

- the capture of Allied fuel reserves. The German forces only had fuel for about a third of the way to Antwerp.

In addition, the attack would have to take place in particularly bad weather conditions, so as to prevent allied reconnaissance, defence and aerial counter-attack operations.

<u>The epilogue to the battle</u>

The weather improved on 23rd December. The allied air force began its counter-attack on the Axis troops, on the roads and in the fields. It bombed the German logistics supply lines and restored supply to their own forces on the ground. The outcome of the Battle of the Bulge, one of the bloodiest battles of the Second World War, determined once and for all, who the winners and losers would be.

On 7th January 1945, Hitler ordered the withdrawal of German forces from Arden. Germany had lost a large part of its last reserves of men and weapons. At the request of Churchill, Joseph Stalin would order the start of the final attack by the Soviet forces on Germany; bringing forward the final offensive on the eastern front to 12th January. It was not long to go until the end of the Second World War.

<u>Applying this example to the business environment</u>

The strategy consists of choosing where to compete. In this case, the choice was to take Antwerp. In the case of insurers, the decision of where to compete involves, besides the geographical perspective, the business sector and the customer segments.

With regards to tactics, the terrain was good for a very fast attack, using available ground forces. Similarly, in the business environment, after determining the strategy, available resources must be aligned (human, financial, technological, and others), with a view to its implementation.

5B) Strategy definition

The key elements to preparing a corporate strategy are the attractiveness of the business and the competitive position of the insurer. Insurers must be in businesses that are attractive and in which they have a good competitive position.

From this point of view, a business is attractive if it has:

- a transaction turnover that is sufficiently large to generate the revenue required to cover the insurer's costs and to create value for the entities with whom it is involved;

- good profit margins, which despite being a characteristic of the business sector, also depend on the business model and the skills of the insurer;

- growth rates that ensure value is created, in the medium/long term, for shareholders, customers, employees, distribution channels and other stakeholders.

The business will be all the more attractive the larger these three dimensions become (turnover, margin and growth), measured within a period of three years, but subject to annual review. In moderately attractive competitive fields, an analysis of the three dimensions must be complemented by a study of synergies with the other businesses in the insurance company.

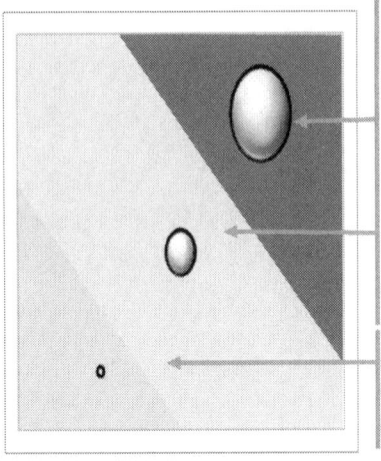

High attractiveness and competitive advantages:

- High volume of sales, growth rate and profit margin
- Better than competitors on Critical Success Factors (CSF)

Average attractiveness:

- The volume of sales, growth rate and profit margins are not high nor too low and competitive position does not stand out
- Only constitutes a valid option if there are significant synergies with other segments where the insurer does business.

Reduced attractiveness or without competitive advantages:

- Low sales volume, growth rate or profit margin or
- Worse than competitors on CSF

Figure 21: The attractiveness of the market segments

However, attractiveness is an average value leaving each insurer in a more or less competitive position in the insurance business.

All activities developed by the insurer are important and if they were not they would be removed. However, some of these activities are particularly important in determining the insurer's competitive position, by what are called "critical success factors" or CSF.

Nothing short of excellence is required in activities decisive to customer choice. Any point scored above or below that of its competitors will determine the strength of the insurer's competitive position and therefore its success.

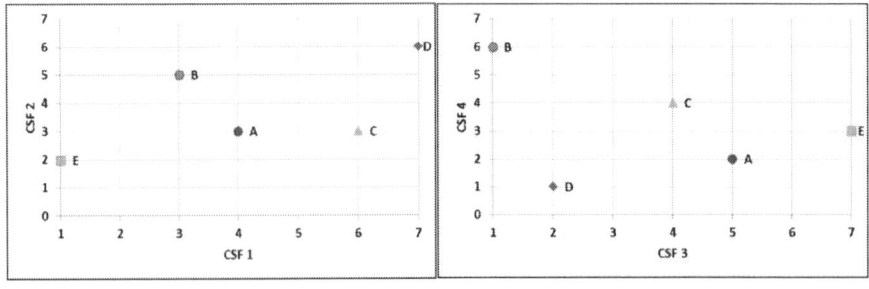

Figure 22: Map of insurer competitive position within the critical success factors

Assuming that the insurance business has four critical success factors (presented in tables as CSF1, CSF2, CSF3 and CSF4), the competitive position of insurer A against its four competitors (B, C, D and E), is determined using the formula:

> Competitive Position A = [ØA - Ø(A, B, C, D, E)) / (Ø(A, B, C, D, E) * 100

Equation 4: Quantification of the competitive position

In this case, it would be:

> Competitive Position A = (14/4-75/20)/(75/20)*100 =
> = (3,5–3,75)/3,75*100 = - 6,67

The competitive position of insurer A is negative, strongly penalised by its performance in CSF 4 and CSF 2, where its performances are negative (respectively, 2 and 3 on a scale of 7).

It is important to avoid other activities (which are not "critical success factors") from becoming problematic. Their performance does not need to be exceptional because the customer does not take them into consideration when making a decision; however, they cannot be negative to the extent that, although not decisive factors, they affect the impression the customer has of the insurance or the insurer (becoming *bottlenecks*).

Documentation the customer receives at the time of purchasing the insurance is an example of this type of factor: although not being decisive in the customer's choice of insurance, if no documentation is received on time, the customer may refuse to take out the insurance.

These are the theories on which business strategy is built and they serve as a conceptual basis for ideas on strategy.

No strategy will succeed if the leading competitors know about it beforehand, so models for building business strategy are no more than a tool in the insurer's strategic development.

The success of a good strategy depends on the ability of the company's managers to adapt the basic theoretical exercise to environmental conditions using their know-how, imagination, experience and creativity, seeking new, attractive business opportunities in which they are likely to achieve a good competitive position.

5B1) Distribution as a strategic business variable

Distribution is extremely important to the insurance business. The model described above can be reconfigured to incorporate it.

Combining:

- a map of the segments selected, which include the geographical area and sector of activity, based on the average value generated by the customer and the growth potential of the same;
- a map of distribution channels, defined by the value generated by the channel and its growth rate,

helps, in general, to predict the strategic guidelines to follow in different customer / channel combinations.

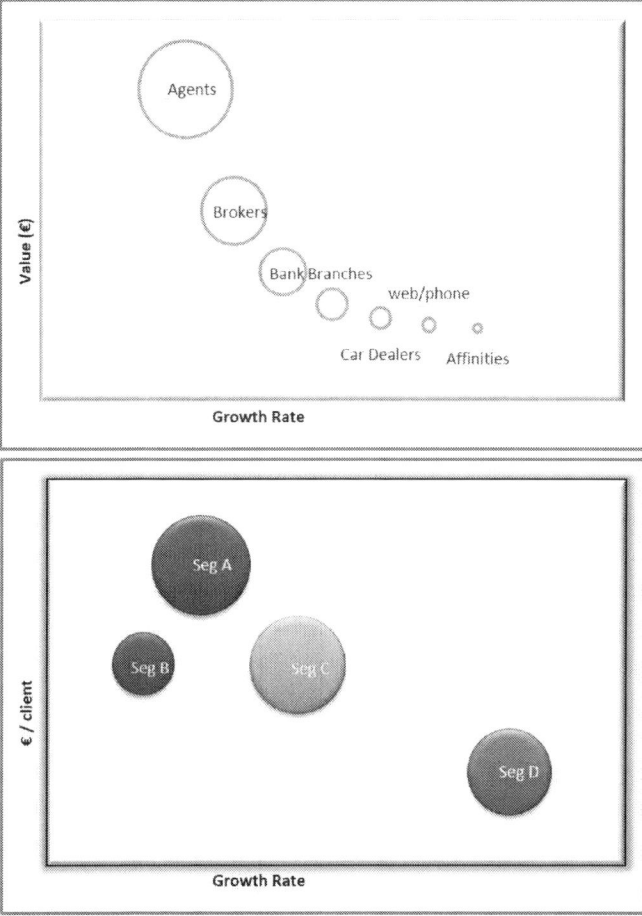

Figure 23: Illustrative maps of segments and distribution channels

The approaches in each of the competitive fields are as follows:

- retention where the generated value is high, but growth is low;

- development in mean value and growth;

- more dynamic measures in situations where the value generated is low but the growth potential is high.

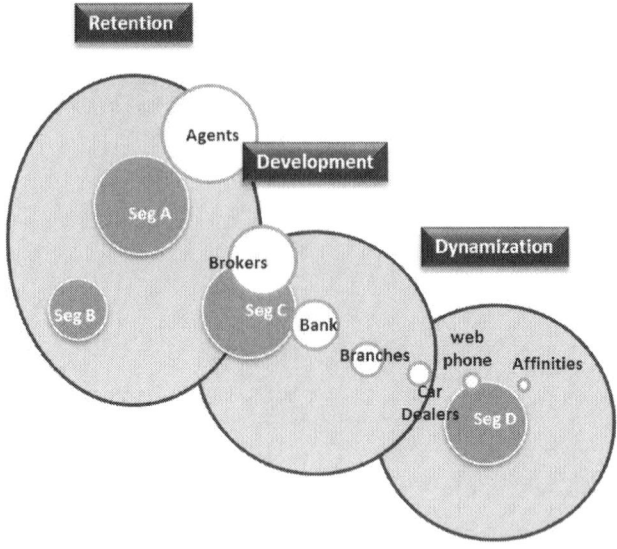

Figure 24: Illustrative representation of strategic priorities in the binomial "segment/channel"

5C) Monitoring the competition

An analysis of competition is decisive insofar as insurer success depends on bringing more satisfaction to its customers and agents than its competitors. It is, therefore, a barometer of the insurer's competitive ability.

The performance considered in absolute terms is relatively less important, taking into account that customer decisions are based on choosing the best available option, taking evoked brands into consideration.

The information for monitoring the competition must be systematically arranged at three levels:

- identifying the structural characteristics of competitors;

- assessing competitive performance, in particular the main strengths and weaknesses of each insurer in relation to the imaginary average of the sector and to the main competitors;

- describing and extrapolating the underlying strategic objectives of strategic moves, namely the underlying goals and reasons behind each initiative.

Monitoring competitors

The market leader and the major competitors[13] must be monitored, observed and analysed. The achievement of this analysis is based on developing two types of document: the insurer's data sheets and the list of relevant moves.

The insurer's data sheets (indicated in figure 25), are completed every six months, identifying the essential elements of each competitor and taking into consideration:

- macro-characterisation, containing information such as legal status, description of key shareholders and the geographical areas of operation.

- main performance indicators;

- description of the main marketing initiatives, such as:

    o the opening or closure of a point of sale;

    o promotions and campaigns or the allocation of sponsorships;

    o the launch, revival or discontinuation of certain types of insurance.

- The strengths and weaknesses of each competitor, involving the people responsible in the different areas of the insurer's operation,

---

[13] Competitors with market shares close to the insurer and that are developing similar strategies in terms of geographical action areas, target customers and distribution channels.

generating an overall, clear perception, of the main opportunities and threats, when compared to each competitor.

Figure 25: Simplified characterisation of competitors

The second type of document that completes the analysis of the competition is the list of relevant moves. This document contains the theme of important events that have occurred in the previous three months.

Responsibility for preparing this observation should be allocated to marketing. Several studies on the competitor, produced by different departments within the structure, should be avoided. Each department should analyse its own indicators, which will necessarily refer to the sector, and that will become part of this document, in order to create a comprehensive picture of each competitor.

At the end of this process, the company must have the necessary information to identify:

- Which insurance companies have the best performance in each critical success factor and why these insurers are better than the others?
- Which critical success factors represent the strong points of our insurer and how these strengths can be exploited?
- Which critical success factors represent the weak points of our insurer and how these weaknesses can be amended?
- What are the weaknesses of each competitor and how these vulnerabilities can be exploited?
- What differences exist between customer segments, particularly the most important for the topics concerned?
- What are the development trends of each insurer?

5D) The fundamental metrics of marketing projects

The return on marketing investment, in its simplest form, is reflected in the cost / benefit of marketing projects. This concept is fundamental because:

- it shows the impact of each marketing initiative in the results of the insurer, distinguishing those that work from those that do not, and leading to the necessary conclusions that will make the operation increasingly more effective;
- insurers need to know the value they generate for all entities related to their business.

Almost from the start, there has been a lack of accuracy in assessing market investments. We know investment is necessary, although aware that a relevant part of the investment is wasted. Companies accept this situation as if it were inevitable, which is wrong, particularly in the terms and on the scale it occurs.

There may be several reasons for not calculating return on investments in market initiatives, such as:

- fear of disclosing less positive results, exposing the vulnerabilities of people and departments;

- inertia and lack of initiative;

- absence of appropriate tools for the purpose;

- a lack of know-how on the best way to do this.

Inaccuracy in assessing returns on marketing projects is justified by a lack of knowledge on marketing function. Justifying and supporting investment decisions based on vague, inaccurate and dogmatic arguments is unsustainable.

As with other business operations, it is essential to apply measurable techniques in assessing investments made in marketing and strategic customer management, such as:

- Net Present Value;

- Payback;

- Internal Rate of Return.

These techniques must be analysed according to scenarios (favourable, intermediate or unfavourable), estimating the respective probabilities of their occurring, and then their expected impact.

There are specific investment indicators for assessing investment in marketing projects that should always be taken into account. The essentials are:

- variation in sales turnover, growth rates and insurer margins, customer segments and distribution channels;

- variation in the level of customer, agent and employee satisfaction.

6) Marketing strategies in the insurance sector

According to the original concept of marketing, the marketing process is divided into two phases:

- definition of the value proposal, corresponding to strategic marketing;

- distribution and communication of value or tactical marketing.

Figure 26: Marketing as a means of value creation

The underlying concept is that the value offered to the customer is the result of the cost / benefit balance:

- benefits are gained, essentially, by transferring risks to an external entity (risk products), or by managing savings (in financial and pension products).

- costs that the customer has to bear in the purchase of insurance are monetary and non-monetary:
    - main monetary costs are associated with payment of the insurance premium. This value depends on the options selected, such as, the deductible, the sums insured or the range of cover.
    - non-monetary costs are the time, energy and fatigue associated with the search and selection of the best product, as well as the psychological costs related to the risk associated with this choice.

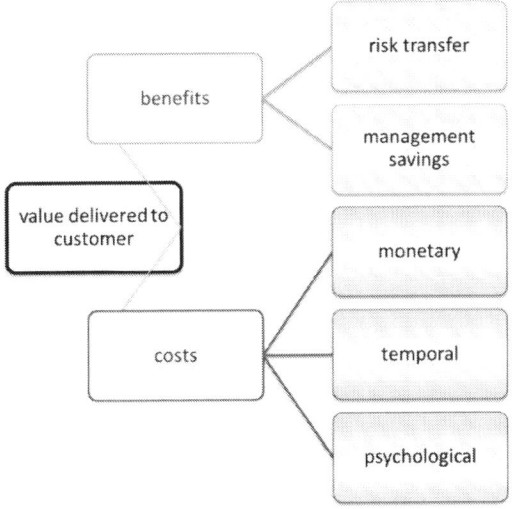

Figure 27: Model of value creation

Consequently the value delivered may be increased in two ways:

- by increasing benefits, or at least to more than costs;
- by lowering costs, or at least to less than benefits.

Insurers must put in place the conditions for developing innovative cost reduction and benefit increase processes, for their customers and business partners.

> To encourage new ideas events should be held where those concerned can discuss a topic with a pre-defined agenda and goal. The best solutions are the result of what participants think about new information and opinions, followed by the opportunity for an exchange of knowledge, experiences and points of view.
>
> Brainstorming sessions, at which employees can speak freely on a specific topic, are not the best approach to create innovative solutions to business challenges, once this technique assumes that:

- the right side of the human brain is responsible for creative, artistic and intuitive skills;

- the left side responds to analytical, logical and rational capabilities.

The perspective that Ideas are created in the right side of the brain while the left side remains passive, is incorrect. This understanding of how the human brain operates is out-dated. The current knowledge of neuroscience is based on the concept of "intelligent memory", according to which the two sides of the brain do not work independently.

In fact, the human brain collects, processes and stores information. Faced with a certain problem or challenge, the brain compares the new information, which it has saved, generating a new conclusion; in other words, a thought or an idea. In this way the intelligent memory combines analysis and rationality with intuition and emotion.

This is why many ideas come to mind at times when the brain is not focused on one problem, as happens in brainstorming processes, but when it is free from other types of problem and concern.

6A) Customer segmentation

The phase of forming the concept of value, or of strategic marketing, begins with customer segmentation, after which the targets are selected and the positioning of the insurance company is established.

Business segmentation consists of grouping customers who share certain similar characteristics, but who differ from other groups of customers. These characteristics are the criteria of segmentation.

Segmentation is a fundamental aspect of customer management because it helps throw light on complex markets that have a wider range of needs and choices.

In the past, there were companies that were successful in applying the mass marketing model (mass production of standardised products, distributed and promoted in the same way for all customers). Because they incurred in fewer costs, lower prices could be charged, or they enjoyed higher profit margins. Currently, this approach leads to failure, because mass produced products have such basic characteristics that they are unable to satisfy all types of customer, and end up by never fully satisfying any customer.

Segmentation is important because insurers need to identify the customers whom they can serve far better than their competitors. In today's markets it is becoming increasingly difficult to bear the costs of non-segmentation because of the impact it has on developing proposals that customers do not accept, as well as the impact of the most profitable customers leaving the insurer.

These segmentation criteria are the factors used to distinguish between customers and to place them in same-type groups. The main segmentation criteria fall into the following categories:

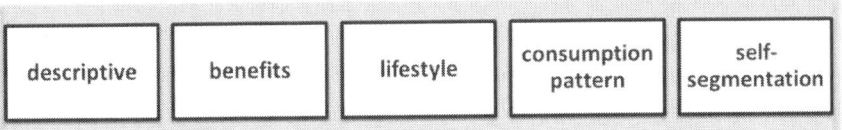

Figure 28: Segmentation criteria

Many times, several criteria are combined in hybrid modes of segmentation.

6A1) Descriptive Factors

The main descriptive segmentation criteria are the following:

- geography, separating customers by factors such as regions, size of city, population density or climate.

    The underlying concept to these criteria is that entities from the same geographic area share the same behavioural patterns, the same needs and desires, which differ from customers in other regions. In the case of crop insurance, for example, customers are segmented according to the climate of the regions in which they live.

- sensitivity to marketing measures the level and type of reaction customers have to marketing stimuli triggered by the insurer.

Among the descriptive criteria, the following only applies to individuals, persons, private entities or families:

- Demography covers social and economic criteria, in particular age, generation, gender, marital status, income, education and occupation.

Gender has always been one of the most used segmentation variables but in recent years gender distinction is less common and customers of both genders are contacted. Marketing is affected by the fact that both partners in a partnership are work individuals. Women, for example, are no longer easily accessible by traditional means of communication. Also male home-workers, many of whom live alone, are becoming an increasingly important segment of the insurance business.

Generation remains an important segmentation criterion. People born post-1990s live attached to the Internet, smartphones and digital social media for almost everything. Soon this new generation of customers will not relate to insurers unless there is interactive transaction and information is always available on devices with Internet access. It is a major break with the way business has been done until now and the way companies and society interact.

Insurance marketing faces the tremendous challenge of providing a services that will meet the needs of customers from different generations, such as the baby-boomers (people who were born post-Second World War) and the interconnected (the younger sector born in the last decade of the twentieth century). These different generations perceive processes and insurance solutions in totally different ways.

The baby-boomers date from before the mass use of computers and Internet. Many of these people are not computer literate, and as such prefer to deal with agents and paper based processes.

The interconnected generation is different in that it is more materialistic and realistic than previous generations, unable to do anything without computers, smartphones or Internet. This younger generation also tends to live for much longer at home with their parents.

This generation finds it difficult to understand why there are so many papers involved in transactions. The relationship with the insurer should be based on the Internet and interactivity at all times. A major change in the way business is done and in how companies and society interact is required for this generation. It is a generation that looks for the best quality-price solution, and it undermines the role of agents because this generation usually seek its own advice.

Age and income are two frequently used variables but can cause mistakes:

- o Age, because often chronological age and psychological age do not coincide;
- o Income, because often those on a high income tend to minimise it and those on a low income tend to maximise it. On the other hand, income only indicates the ability (or inability) of a customer to pay for certain insurance, regardless of wanting or needing the insurance.
- Social and cultural variables, involving the life cycle analysis of families, social class and culture.

The life cycle of families is based on the assumption that families go through similar stages in their formation, growth and separation, and the specific needs of each of these stages can be identified. Generally the following stages are identified:

Family Life Cycle	Income level and type of purchases	Examples of insurance needs
young dependents	• No own income. • Education, technological equipment and leisure.	• long-term capital growth investment funds • saving solutions
young professionals	• Limited income but large amplitude of spending. • First home, automobile, clothing and travel.	• Motor and home.
young families	• Increasing returns. • Larger house, durable goods (appliances and furniture), leisure and articles for children.	• Health, personal accident and personal liability
mature families	• Incomes have the highest value. • products that confer greater social status and to the children	• Pension plan and travel
retirees and pensioners	• Income decrease sharply. • Health and security	• Nurse assistance and workers' compensation

Figure 29: Phases in the life cycle of families

Social class is normally determined using a weighted index of socio-economic variables, such as income, education and occupation. This variable covers a wide range of differences depending on context: the upper class in a rich region of a developed country differs entirely from the upper class in a poor area of a developing country. On the other hand, in certain environments, more importance is attached to education and profession than to income, whilst in others the opposite is true, and more importance is attached to the material wealth of individuals.

Culture is particularly important in international business management. This variable characterises customers based on factors such as nationality, race and religion, given that members of the same culture tend to share the same values, beliefs and habits.

Lastly, there are descriptive criteria that apply only to collective customers (companies and non-profit making organisations). The most common being:

- the legal nature of the organisation that essentially distinguishes between public, private, cooperative and mutual companies;

- the type of economic activity, identifiable by means of an official statistical code of activities;

- the dimension, measured using variables such as business turnover and number of employees;

- the age of the organisation.

With respect to Sole Traders, although sharing some of the characteristics of individuals and companies, their decision models are closer to that of private customers than companies. This does not invalidate the application of descriptive business criteria to these customers when they purchase insurance that meets a collective need.

Preferably, these customers must be segmented and managed as a group separate from individuals and from companies.

6A2) Benefits

There are several reasons why customers purchase insurance, and so they receive different types of benefit when they take out insurance cover.

Using this method of segmentation, customers are classified according to the type of benefit they acquire, the result of combining the type of the actual insurance and the customer's sense of values.

Contrary to what happens in other types of business, most customers receive benefits that are real, measurable, concrete or psychological when they purchase an insurance, but they rarely seek social benefits from possessing or consuming a particular brand.

6A3) Life Style

Lifestyle is a variable used increasingly. Classification here focuses on the customer activities, interests and opinions.

The factors used are psychological, based on an analysis of the internal or intrinsic characteristics of the individual customer, including customer needs, motivations, personality, perceptions and attitudes.

Demographic, socio-economic and life style variables are often used together.

6A4) Consumption patterns

Criteria associated with consumption patterns are distinguished from all others because they are related to the purchase and consumption patterns of insurance. Three examples of criteria associated with the nature of consumption are:

- intensity of use, distinguishes customers according to the number and value of insurance policies purchased.

Many customers tend to purchase only compulsory insurance, meaning that one of the challenges faced by insurers is to increase the amount of insurance owned by their customers, leading them to purchase optional products. On the other hand, there are many opportunities to increase customer value by selling additional coverage to a customer's existing insurance policy by updating and increasing the sums insured.

- brand loyalty distinguishes customers according to *share-of-wallet*, or in other words, the percentage share of their business out of the insurer's total business. There are customers who value the diversification of their portfolios with several insurers ("do not put all your eggs in one basket", they say), whilst others prefer to concentrate insurance in just one insurance company (easier management of their contracts, increase their bargaining power, or simply at the agent's suggestion). The insurers' challenge is to:

- o convince customers that there are advantages in having all their insurances with the same insurer;

- o demonstrate that the insurer is the customer's best option.

- The occasion of use criterion, distinguishes customers according to the time at which they purchase the insurance. Season-led sales are very important in insurance cover for hunting, crops or travel. The challenge for insurers is to counteract the seasonality of insurance by:

  - o increasing sales at other times of the year;

  - o identifying other times when the customer could consume certain insurance, such as savings insurances for a child's birthday.

In dealing with claims, insurers must also manage the seasonality of different types of risk, e.g. over the Christmas festive season more claims are made due to:

- o personal injuries cause by a trip or fall;

- o frozen pipes affecting the home;

- o health, namely flu, heart attacks and other diseases.

6A5) Self-segmentation

The emergence of social networks created the phenomenon of self-segmentation. The principle is that individuals using the social media access websites and visit virtual communities, with which they identify and find interesting. No one knows customers better than they do themselves, so knowing the areas they access provides information that is very effective for:

- the purchase procedure;

- consumption patterns;

- the likelihood of fraud;

- strengths and weaknesses of the insurer and its offer, as well as opportunities for improvement.

This knowledge also allows the insurer to interact with the different groups to which customers relate, and consequently to improve the customer experience. From an analysis of customer preferences, the insurer can format its sites, proposals and communications to suit customer preferences in browsing, consulting and purchasing, tailoring the experience to the characteristics, profile and interests of each customer.

6A6) Validating segments

The segmentation criteria that best describe customers are the most difficult to identify. For individual customers, geographical characteristics or gender are easily determined but are very limited in explaining behaviour; on the contrary, psychological characteristics are much more difficult to identify, but distinguish far more between the different customer profiles.

After applying segmentation criteria, the relevance of the resulting segments must be confirmed. To this end, four conditions should be checked:

- identifiable, enabling characterisation of customers;

- sufficient, covering a sufficient number of customers to make the investment in developing a specific value proposal worthwhile;

- stable or in a growth status, in order to ensure they are sustainable in the medium to long term;

- accessible, in terms of means of communication and costs, because cost-effective targets must be met.

Lastly, the following fundamental information is required to describe segments:

- the number of individuals each contains;
- the average value of each customer;
- the average number and value of insurances held;
- the type and amount of costs generated, in particular those associated with claims and the distribution channel;
- average age;
- payment methods;
- the frequency of purchases and how recently made;
- the number and type of campaigns in which they are involved;
- trends in migration between segments.

The emergence of new customer segments, associated with more competitive conditions and technological innovation, has led to the micro-segmentation of the market. Insurers have been developing solutions to serve increasingly smaller niches of customers.

6A7) Implementing segmentation

The most basic approach to implementing segmentation in insurance companies that measure the value of their customers consists of the MVP (*marketing to value and potential*) approach. This model makes a general distinction between high, medium, low and negative categories, which helps determine objectives in developing customers to higher value levels.

Despite the importance of this step getting to know customers and dealing with them in different ways, it does not explain how to increase customer value. Consequently, customer value must be crossed with other types of variables such as life-cycle (see figure 30), purchase profiles, as well as using the variable yet to be exploited by most insurers, which is life-style.

		Family Life Cycle					
		Young dependent	young professional	Young families	Mature families	Retired & Pensioners	
Client Value (€)	A > 1000						€ (%) # clients (%)
	B 500 - 1000						€ (%) # clients (%)
	C 150 - 500						€ (%) # clients (%)
	D 0 - 150						€ (%) # clients (%)
	E < 0						€ (%) # clients (%)

Figure 30: Illustrative segmentation matrix resulting from crossing value and family life cycle

		Channel					
		Direct writing	Agents	Brokers	Bancassurance	Other	
Client Value (€)	A > 1000€						€ (Y) % € (Y+3) %
	B 500€ - 1000€						€ (Y) % € (Y+3) %
	C 150€-500€						€ (Y) % € (Y+3) %
	D 0€-150€						€ (Y) % € (Y+3) %
	E < 0€						€ (Y) % € (Y+3) %

Figure 31: Segmentation matrix resulting from customer value and distribution channel

This figure shows the current relative and future increase (over three years), highlighting the segments with the highest potential for growth according to colour.

Using these elements insurers can establish a development plan for each segment, which should include:

- financial opportunity for the next 12 months and 3 years;

- main theme of the approach to the segment;

- objectives to be achieved in each segment;

- standard of service to be made available;

- main marketing actions to be developed.

6A8) Consequences of segmentation

Segmentation is indispensable for efficient customer management as it allocates resources to customers according to their value, and increases their overall value.

This process is also very important for distribution, because insurers will have an understanding that will help them develop stronger, more profitable and longer lasting relationships with end customers.

In the case of those customers that generate negative results, segmentation will mean they no longer benefit from the same standards of service provided to more profitable customers.

Ceasing to work with low value customers by presenting them with prohibitive costs or making the business process more difficult for them, makes sense from an economic point of view, although the concept contradicts the insurer's social obligations of solidarity and reciprocity.

However, this form of solidarity has to be assumed as a social cost for all. Other insurer duties, such as providing insurance solutions at the lowest possible cost, ensuring good working conditions for its employees and adequate returns on the capital invested by shareholders, may only be achieved if the destruction of value caused by customers who adopt high risk behaviour is controlled.

The following tables illustrate the foundations for the development of a matrix of individual and collective customer segmentation.

		Low potential value		High potential value	
		Low profitability	High profitability	Low profitability	High profitability
Family Life Cycle	young dependents	Segment A1	Segment A2	Segment A3	Segment A4
	young professionals	Segment B1	Segment B2	Segment B3	Segment B4
	young families	Segment C1	Segment C2	Segment C3	Segment C4
	mature families	Segment D1	Segment D2	Segment D3	Segment D4
	retirees and pensioners	Segment E1	Segment E2	Segment E3	Segment E4
Soho (small office / home office)		Segment S1	Segment S2	Segment S3	Segment S4

Figure 32: Basis for the development of individual customer segmentation

		Low potential value		High potential value	
		Low profitability	High profitability	Low profitability	High profitability
Business sector	manufacturing	Segment A1	Segment A2	Segment A3	Segment A4
	commerce	Segment B1	Segment B2	Segment B3	Segment B4
	services	Segment C1	Segment C2	Segment C3	Segment C4
	industry	Segment D1	Segment D2	Segment D3	Segment D4
Non-profit		Segment S1	Segment S2	Segment S3	Segment S4

Figure 33: Basis for the development of business customer segmentation

Insurers must develop a matrix that equates customer characteristics to marketing tactics. The insurer should reward higher value customers by providing them with a priority quality service and other benefits that make them feel special.

6B) Target selection

The second phase of value conceptualisation, or strategic marketing, after customer segmentation, consists of identifying customers that insurers want to target.

The insurer should select the segments that are attractive and the ones in which they have a competitive advantage over other insurers, as referred to in the chapter "The strategy definition".

6C) Positioning

The third phase of value conceptualisation, or strategic marketing, after customer segmentation and identification of target segments, is to define the insurer's position.

To determine the competitive position of the insurer, the areas must be defined where the insurer will compete with other insurers to attract the business of customers within the target segment.

In selecting these areas, the insurer has chosen the competitive terrain in which to do business. In adopting its position the insurer determines the best way to exploit its competitive advantages, which consist of areas in which its strong points coincide with the critical success factors of the business.

It is essential that target customers recognise that the insurer's performance is excellent or, at least, it is the best of all competitors, in critical success factors.

For simplicity, four basic positioning factors are identified: low price, high quality, additional services and innovation (as shown in figure 34):

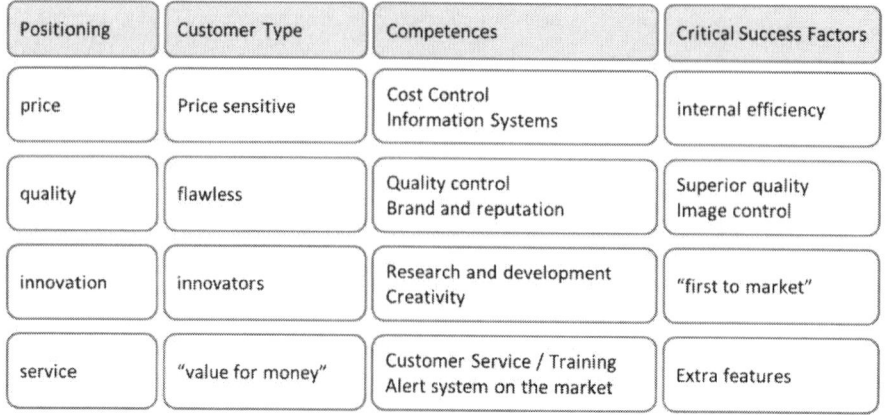

Figure 34: Positioning options

The different positioning areas facilitate access to different types of customer. The insurer must have the appropriate skills for each distinguishing factor, and be the best in the respective critical success factors. The whole insurance company must be aligned in mobilising around that factor to ensure that the customer's perception of performance in this area suggests it is the best in the market.

If, for example, the insurer is positioned as "low price", all employees, in all tasks, must seek to minimise the insurer's costs.

The number of customer choice factors in the positioning of the insurer, has the following implications:

- Positioning as a single factor:

    o The benefits are ease of communication and being more objective in the distinction between what is essential and what is accessory in achieving success.

    o The main disadvantage is the restricted size of the target segment, given that it only encompasses customers that value that specific factor, so that if there is a competitor performing better in this, the insurer will not have any competitive advantage.

- Positioning in two or three factors seems to be the most suitable option for insurers in general;

- Positioning in four or more factors is usually not advisable because besides being more difficult for customers in the target segment to associate the brand with the various areas of insurer excellence, it entails making large investments in scattered areas with less room for gains from synergy.

Despite the number of factors supporting the positioning of insurers, the following problems are frequent:

- perception of inconsistency and incoherence as a result of the insurer's aim to distinguish itself in incompatible areas;

- positioning is based on a factor that is insufficiently valued by customers, leading to the perception of a deficient quality-price ratio that makes customers unwilling to pay a higher value for attributes they do not value;

- the performance of the insurer in the distinguishing factor is not sufficiently superior to that of other competitors, and the customer fails to see the benefits of buying the insurance.

In any one of these cases, it is not evident to the customer that the choice of insurance is the best option, which will prevent them from purchasing it.

Although insurers have to select a limited number of factors that distinguish them from competitors, performance in other areas is also important. For a customer to select a given type of insurance, that insurance must be excellent or, at the least, better than that of competitors in terms of critical success factors. Furthermore, the insurer must also demonstrate an acceptable or satisfactory performance in other fields.

To refer back to the case of the insurer positioned in the "low price" category, if the agent does not deal with this customer in a caring and friendly manner the offer of a cheaper insurance will not serve its purpose.

7) Marketing tactics in the insurance sector

Tactics are no less important than strategy, although they depend on it. Developing tactics, that is, the way in which the company organises and structures itself to implement the strategy, depends directly on strategic options. Poor business performance can result from:

- wrong strategies;
- good strategies that are poorly executed;
- inability to implement tactics;
- inconsistency between the various aspects of tactics;
- tactics inconsistent with the strategy.

Both the strategic and tactical components, that are coherent and consistent, and adequately implemented, are necessary for the insurer to achieve its objectives.

On the subject of marketing, the tactics refer to the variables of the *marketing mix*: product, price, distribution and communication. However, this combination, initially developed and applied to the industrial sector, has a less positive effect when applied to financial services. The way to overcome this limitation is to associate three other variables to the traditional marketing-*mix*, which are: people, physical evidence and processes.

The basic aspects in defining marketing tactics are:

- The balance and coherence in combining and implementing its seven variables.

    If, for example, the intention is to sell over the phone, the insurance should be simple and inexpensive, and promotion must be widespread. However, if access is via the broker channel, products must be complete, comprehensive and sophisticated, and communication must be more focused on the sales force.

- The effect of synergies between the variables should be duly identified and exploited.

7A) The insurance product

Customers are fundamental because it is through profitable customers that revenue is generated, helping Insurance companies grow and prosper. However, these financial flows occur through the purchasing of insurance products.

Insurers must have data that enables them to monitor the level at which each product is performing its role, throwing light on whether it is satisfying the needs for which it was designed.

The main product management indicators are those that relate to the strategic management of the insurer, namely sales volume, growth rates and profit margins, determined by the market segments in which the company operates. However, the insurer and its products can be either good or bad, not only due to their own merits or lack of, but also due to alternatives offered by competitors, so that the insurer needs to know of other proposals available on the market.

7A1) Basic understanding of the insurance product

Fundamental ideas on the insurance product, particularly on "classical" insurance, those in which the risk component is more pronounced, are as follows:

- the policy covers certain specific risks that are clearly identified and detailed in the policy conditions (general, special and particular);

- if a random event occurs that is covered by an insurance contract, the insurer is obliged to compensate in accordance with the provision of the contract;

- the insurer is obliged to make the contract official in writing and deliver it to the policy-holder, duly signed and dated;

- an insurance only takes effect when it has been paid, given that the initial premium or, in the case of payment in instalments, the initial instalment, must be paid at the time of signing the contract. If these payments are not made, the contract does not come into force;

- the insurer must notify the policy-holder in writing, of the amount, method and location of payment, with the minimum advance laid down by law (usually 30 days), in relation to the payment due date of the premium or fraction thereof;

- if the customer does not pay the subsequent annuities or the next instalment, the contract is not extended;

- the policy-holder, the insured person, or the beneficiary, must notify the insurer of a claim within the period stated in the contract, usually up to eight days following the date of its occurrence.

- lastly, insurance is prohibited for the following risks:

    - criminal liability, penalties or disciplinary sanctions;

    - abduction, kidnapping and other crimes against personal freedom;

    - the possession or carriage of narcotics or drugs, the consumption of which is prohibited;

    - the death of any child under the age of 14 or any individual whose mental or psychic ability deems them unfit to care for themselves.

From here on, everything (or almost everything), can be insured and there are even examples of extraordinary risk covers, many of them placed with the insurance broker, Lloyds of London, such as the fingers of the guitarist Jeff Becks, the legs of Mariah Carey or alien abductions.

A very important and sensitive issue relates to discriminatory practices in the signing, execution and termination of contracts, due to the disability or increased health risk of the policy-holder or insured person. This type of discrimination may be in violation of the principle of equality. However, as long as the evaluation, selection and acceptance of risks are strictly backed by statistics and are objectively demonstrated, they are allowed and accepted. Consequently, there is a grey area of ambiguity arising out of situations of disability or increased health risk that change the risk assessment, in a statistically verifiable manner.

<u>Insurable risks</u>

For a certain phenomenon to be considered a risk, three conditions must be met:

- it is uncertain and random;
- it generates a potential loss;
- it is measurable and quantifiable.

For a given risk to be insurable, the evaluation of potential losses must be quantifiable in financial terms, therefore from an insurer perspective, the risk is defined as the probability of occurrence of a given random event that is liable to generate a given financial loss. Insurable risks are classified in terms of their financial impact, the magnitude of their potential effects and their variability.

There are two types of financial impact on risks:

- pure risks, when their occurrence only causes material loss, such as, fire, theft or water damage;

- speculative risks, which are liable to generate material gains as well as losses. This is the case of certain life insurance policies, with applications in equity funds.

The extent of the potential effects of a risk can be:

- Delimited or limited, if it is confined to a small group of people or objects such as a motor accident or home burglary;

- Colossal or extended, if the potential damages affect a large number of people or goods, as in the case of an epidemic, an earthquake or rise in interest rates.

The variability of how risks are characterised also defines them:

- static risks are those whose definition and description remain unchanged for many years, such as fire, theft or tsunami;

- dynamic risks are those that have been redefined over the years, due to the economic and social development of mankind, and that are likely to continue to evolve. These are, for example, cases of public environmental liabilities and work-related accidents.

7A2) The fundamental functions of insurance

If insurance did not exist, developed societies could not operate as we know them. The immense importance of insurance comes as a result of its irreplaceable role, particularly the following:

- allowing people and companies to transfer risks that threaten their personal well-being and property to an external entity, and one that specialises in risk management (an insurer or reinsurer);

- serving as a vehicle for promoting savings, through two mechanisms:

  - in the application of financial resources for personal and property protection, embodied in the insurance premium payment;

  - in the creation and sale of solutions for the application of savings, taking into account the characteristics and profiles of each customer. Insurance companies offer a wide range of savings insurance, from the more conservative options that prefer insurance without risk and with guaranteed rates and sums insured, to those that are more aggressive, that prefer, above all, a potential return on the application.

- encouraging economic development, which is the result of several combined effects, in particular:

  - freeing funds that, in the case of no insurance existing, customers would have to retain in order to cover the possible occurrence of a claim;

  - guaranteeing bank loans;

  - ensuring the availability of financial resources in order to resume activities affected by a claim;

  - encouraging the adoption of behaviour that reduces the likelihood of a claim occurring.

7A3) Insurance typology

Insurance can be identified according to:

- risks covered, such as fire, health or pension plan;

- insured object, such as motor insurance or leisure craft;

- type of service provided in the event of a claim being made, such as assistance, legal protection or rental insurance.

In terms of typology, there are two large groups of insurance, and these are:

  o material damage, covering risks to objects, intangible goods, loans and other equity rights.

  o personal insurance, when the risks refer to life, health or the physical or psychological integrity of a person or group of persons.

Traditionally, the insurance sector uses risk classification based on insurance lines:

- Non-life insurance. Within this group are the following sub-groups:

  o accident and health, which includes workers' compensation insurance, personal accident insurance and health insurance;

  o property, which besides fire risks, includes all-risk property insurance, commercial and industrial insurance, agricultural, livestock and engineering insurances;

  o motor;

  o transport;

  o third party liability, in particular public, employer, professional and product;

  o other types, including all type of insurance not included under any of the lines mentioned, such as assistance.

- Life insurance that includes:

- protection policies, which cover mainly life and the deterioration of the physical and/or psychological abilities of beneficiaries;

- pension plans, designed to create a savings fund for retirement;

- financial insurance that aims to capitalise applications, usually in the medium to long term.

7A4) The dimensions of the insurance product

The insurance product has three different dimensions:

- legal cover, activated in the case of an event occurring, which is identified and typified in the contract conditions;

- the product that is sold and that, in addition to the policy, includes:

  - the explanation, support and advice on subscribed insurance policy underwritten;

  - other documentation delivered to the customer;

  - customer services.

- the needs that are met are:

  - the peace of mind resulting from the guarantee that if the random phenomenon foreseen in the contract occurs, there will be compensation, which may be monetary or in the form of services (such as the case of a tow truck service under the motor assistance insurance);

  - respect for a legal requirement, as in the case of compulsory work-related accident insurance;

  - property development, when dealing with financial insurances.

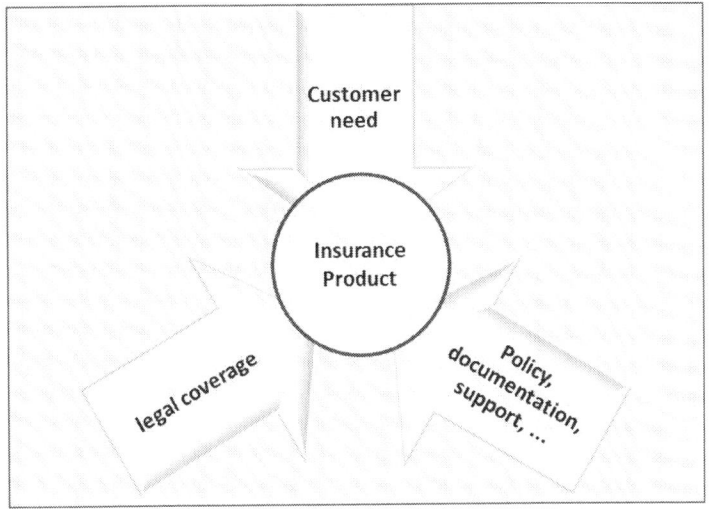

Figure 35: The three dimensions of the insurance product

The insurance product contains these three aspects. However, depending on circumstances and the customer's profile, one dimension may gain precedence over the others.

7A5) Special features of the insurance product

There are three very relevant features to this product, which are:

- The major difficulty customers have in assessing and comparing alternatives, the result of:

    o the product being intrinsically complex in nature, given that it is based on technical and legal clauses that are often long and difficult to interpret (even for professionals in the sector);

    o the existence of many varying solutions to cover the same risks. If, for example home insurance is required, there is a wide range of products to choose from, with different combinations of cover, sums insured, deductibles, exclusions, etc.;

- o the current tendency to bundle policies into insurance solutions, or even more all-embracing offers such as global financial solutions that in addition to the insurance, include banking products.

- The importance of the configuration of the distribution channel. Each distribution channel is aimed and trained to prioritise different components of a given proposal value. For this reason, the insurance has to be designed, configured and formatted according to the specific features of the channel in which it will be placed. Failures often occur in launching insurance because the insurer is unable to communicate throughout all its distribution channels in order to promote the advantages of its proposal compared to those of competitors. This factor is particularly important in a competitive environment in which non-exclusive agents dominate in distribution.

7B) Price definition

The price, which in the insurance business is called the premium, is the only tactical marketing variable that generates revenue. Other variables have a negative impact on insurer results, in respect of profit and loss accounts.

The price is a determining factor for profitability and for insurer's market share. The usual strategic alternatives faced are:

- the focus on high-value customers, where products are sold at higher average premiums, generating higher margins, but with a lower sales turnover and consequently a decreasing market share;

- counting on lower segment value, developing simpler products with fewer cover options and lower sums insured, so as to reduce the average premium of each policy, with a reduction in profit margins, but stimulating both the quantity of policies sold and the market share of the insurance company.

In practice, there is a third way that detects the good risk niches, involving activities and people less frequently affected by claims or making only limited impact claims, which exist in all lines of insurance. Exploiting this type of business means that competitive prices can be applied, and so profits and high turnover are maintained, and consequently, insurer's market share rises. Analytical marketing tools are used to determine precisely which businesses fall into this category.

This approach is often criticised because it does not comply with the principles of solidarity and reciprocity, in which the many should contribute with a little in order to safeguard the unfortunate from the occurrence of random events. This is an important principle, but the supervisory and regulatory bodies must enforce it, guaranteeing that all customers are able to meet their basic insurance needs, in terms of cover and acceptable price.

From an insurer's perspective, it is far more important to safeguard the principle of prevention, rewarding those customers who adopt the correct approach to the risks around them, unlike those who disregard risks and do nothing to prevent them.

The price variable is also very important because it generates perceptions of product quality. Providing insurance at a price significantly lower than that of competitors, for no reason or justification, creates a perception that the price reduction is due to a reduction in the quality of the product. In insurance, as well as in most business sectors, cheaper products are not market leaders.

Nevertheless, the tenuous relationship between customers and insurers when it comes to the purchasing process, leads to overestimating the price as a decision criteria. In the United Kingdom, although a market with its own specific features, there are statistics to show that approximately one-third of customers change their motor insurance for less than a 10% reduction in premium.

7B1) Aspects central to premium management

The following aspects are essential to insurance premium management:

- Costs, in particular those in the sections that follow, consume a substantial part of the insurer's marketing budget, and affect the final price of the insurance:
    - commissions paid to distributors and other acquisition costs;
    - fixed costs, for example, properties used by the insurer;
    - studies and consultancy, often used in the internal restructuring and development of new business;
    - human resources;
    - communications, in all aspects;
    - customer management costs;
    - claims settlement;
    - Fraud. This type of cost is particularly relevant in this business, although it is not a cost directly associated with marketing. Fraud has a significant impact on prices and on insurer results. The competitive ability of insurers is also determined by their skills in dealing with this issue.

- The amount that customers are willing to pay. The study of customer income can be misleading in relation to how much customers are willing to pay. The financial outlay they are willing to make on insurance depends basically on the importance they attach to risk protection. For some customers insurance satisfies a basic need for safety and security, while for others insurance is an accessory because the unlikelihood of risks occurring contrasts with the certainty of paying a policy premium. Customers must be analysed, bearing in mind their characteristics and behaviour, adding information on their income level to cultural, psychological and behavioural aspects, as well as their possession/use of insurance.

- The practices used by the competition also determine premiums that may be applied. All insurers must have a system for monitoring the prices charged by their main competitors. These indications are critical because they determine:

    o the maximum above which insurance prices should not rise;

    o the minimum below which they should not fall, so as not to lose revenue without an increase in competitiveness;

    o the relative position of the insurer and each of its insurance policies compared to the main competitors.

- Legal and regulatory policies, essentially fiscal and para-fiscal charges. The insurance sector deducts a portion of premiums charged to customers to give to services such as fire-fighters, medical emergency services, motor guarantee fund, occupational accidents fund and civil protection, among others. In addition, there are costs incurred with compulsory solvency requirements and capital ratios.

- The need to distinguish the insurance premium from its total cost to the customer. The customer can opt for different combinations of cover, sums insured and deductibles, depending on the risks they decide to cover themselves (self-insurance) and the part that is transferred to the insurer. Each combination has different immediate and future financial impacts. Other aspects that affect the amount customers pay for insurance are:

    o the insurers discount policy;

    o payments made in instalments (with or without additional costs);

- low claims rate incentives, for example, returning part of the net annual results on the policy to the policy holder;

- bonus-malus systems.

There are still other types of cost incurred on expenses not associated with assumed risks, but which Insurance companies reflect in the cost of the policy, such as for issuing and amending contracts.

Lastly, and also relevant, is the cost to the customer of the time and effort spent in getting information, underwriting and managing the policy, which, if not included in the insurance premium, should be carefully assessed, managed and controlled by the insurer due to the impact it has on the customer experience.

- The difficulty in supervising *dumping* practices. The true cost of the insurance cannot be known prior to its expiry. The value of claims is only known long after the premium is defined. However, insurers must have actuarial and statistical elements available that justify their price scales, preventing this type of practice undermining value.

7B2) Definition of the insurance premium

There are five key components to the total insurance premium in the non-life business:

- the pure risk premium that generally represents around 60% to 70% of the total premium;

- costs to the insurer, which tend not to exceed 15% of the insurance premium;

- contingency premiums, which serve to cover extraordinary losses that are not foreseen in available statistical models, can be worth around 5% of the total premium.

- profit margin.

In the insurance business, in addition to technical results that come mainly from adjusting the estimate of the pure risk premium to claims made, there are also financial results. This additional source of results for the insurer is because the insurer holds an advanced premium amount for the time from the claim occurring to the time the indemnity is paid.

Accuracy in calculating insurance premiums is fundamental to the survival of insurers in the medium term, in that:

- very high premiums reduce insurer competitiveness, making it more difficult to gain new business and retain contracts, and this has an effect on the ability of the insurer to cover its fixed costs;

- premiums that are too low generate technical losses, with an impact on insurer solvency.

However, here there is significant potential for innovation. In the case of several products, such as home insurance, the same variables have been used for many years to calculate tariffs. Basically these are:

- location;
- size of building;
- period of occupation;
- construction materials;
- type of construction;
- existence of security systems.

Few marketing areas remain as unchanged as this one for so many years. There are other variables by which Insurance companies could distinguish themselves from competitor proposals, but these have not been put to the test, since it is not usual to devise different solutions. For example, a customer with a no claims bonus on motor insurance is likely to have risk prevention behaviour more likely to prevent a claim occurring in the home than if there were several security systems in place.

Motor insurance rates are another example of the same methods and variables being used for many years, which are basically:

- the area of residence;
- the driver's age;
- the date on the driver's licence;
- the type of vehicle.

The outcome is a less selective rate, which prejudices good customers and benefits bad drivers. Insurance companies that innovate in this field will have a competitive edge over others. Other social, demographic and transactional data should be used to assess these risks, such as:

- the driver's profession;
- the method and average payment times of other contracts;
- other insurances that the customer already holds;
- length of time with the insurer;
- claims history, in all insurance lines.

Methods used to determine the pure risk premium

There are three main methods used to determine the pure risk premium, which differ in their degree of complexity and customisation of the insured object. These three methods are: the valuation of class, the valuation of merit and expert opinions. In addition to these three methods, there are other processes to determine the pure risk premium based on variations of the models presented.

The pure premium, also known as the simple premium, is a reference to which are added costs, discounts and overheads, targeted margins and fiscal and para-fiscal charges, to arrive at the premium customers pay for the policy.

Category valuation

This is the most classical method. It is based on the assumption that the variables that affect the likelihood of a claim occurring, and its severity, will behave similarly in the future as in the past. The pure premium (in other words, the actual risk assessment) is therefore the result of multiplying the average cost of the claim by the probability of its occurrence.

> **Pure Premium = average cost of claim * probability of occurrence**

Equation 5: Pure premium calculation

In some types of insurance, the reference is the pure rate, which is the result of multiplying the frequency of claims by their intensity. The intensity is the ratio of the average cost of over average sums insured, which is the equivalent of the proportion of capital insured that, on average, is consumed in each claim.

> **Pure Premium = pure rate * sums insured**

Merit evaluation

This method consists of re-assessing the category, adjusted to the object or person insured. There are two sub-categories:

- The assignment of characteristics, which adjusts the risk value to the factors involved in the risk and which do not change. This could be an increase or reduction in a housing risk due to the age of the property, the type of construction or the introduction of fire detection systems. In the case of motor insurance, it is the number of years the driver has

held a license or, in the case of health insurance, the age of the insured person.
- The effects of experience consists in calibrating risk assessment with the prior experience of the insured object or person. An example is the application of the *bonus-malus* table depending on the number of claim-free years for the customer.

It is current practice, in all insurance sectors, to analyse how profitable contracts will be, at least taking account of rate and frequency of claims. This should be done fairly regularly, and usually on an annual basis, adjusting the value of the premium to the results of prior experience.

Expert opinions

This is the method used when there is insufficient quantitative or qualitative past history to produce a statistical series for risk determination. There are two types of situation:

- when there are very few insurance types that cover these risks, such as nuclear energy, military weapon industries or aeronautical and space transport;
- when the risks are very recent and their total impact is not known in the medium/long term, such as risks associated with genetically modified plants and animals.

In these cases, the solution is to estimate the likelihood of a claim occurring and its severity, using specialists and companies specialising in the activities involved. These specialists make assessments that are then used to produce statistics on these risks.

In practice, this method contains a far greater degree of uncertainty than the others, in that these evaluations are usually supported by pessimistic probabilities, and so lead to very high premiums, an obvious disadvantage for customers, but safeguarding the insurer from the unknowns associated with them.

7B3) Methods of premium payment

Payment methods used by insurers are directly related to the characteristics of products and the distribution channels used to market them.

The financial products and sales made through banks are mostly linked to direct debit payments, facilitated by the fact that banks control the process of automatic direct debiting of amounts from their customers' accounts.

In several countries, billing through agents is the method most used in non-life insurance. A part of the remuneration of this channel is in the form of commission on collection.

There are some very strong development trends in how insurance payments are made:

- Direct debit systems are becoming more popular for non-life insurance. This payment method has a direct and objective impact on the rate of customer retention, bearing in mind that loss of customers is a concern throughout the whole sector. Insurers should solidly promote direct debit payment with their customers or agents.

    Insurers provide customers who pay by direct debit with benefits, for example paying in instalments (monthly, quarterly or half-yearly), without adding any interest charge.

    Agents have arranged for their commission to be paid by direct debt from customers, although they do not intervene in the actual receipt of payment for these policies.

- Inversely, payment to banks and insurance companies is on the decline as it does not benefit the customer (takes longer and costs more than alternatives), and it is of no interest to agents.

7B4) The time the insurance payment is made

There is a relatively widespread practice of having insurance policies paid in a certain month (usually January) and monthly payments made on a certain day. These times are set according to the internal planning processes of insurance companies. This procedure is not aligned to the characteristics and specific needs of many customers and so is not recommended in the light of marketing philosophy and insurer interests.

Essential in defining the right time to invoice the customer for the insurance policy are:

- the customer's interest, since the customer knows best when the right time is to be charged by the insurance company;

- billing efficiency, ensuring that the arrival of the insurer's bill coincides with the time when the customer is most solvent.

This pro-activity, in not leaving the time the policy is paid for up to chance, can have a very significant effect on insurance payment collection.

Profession, in the case of individual customers, and business sector, in the case of companies, provide some very useful information when customers have indicated a preference as to when they will pay for their insurance.

If, for example, a corporate customer is in the business of summer tourism, it would be inappropriate to schedule payment collection in January (as many insurers do). It would be far better for both the insurer and the customer if the charge were made when liquidity is higher, which would be during the summer.

In the case of civil servants, whose payday is known, the insurer would be advised to pay bill on the day following pay-day.

7B5) The decision to increase or reduce the insurance premium

Taking account of the insurer's goals, the option on rates means:

- higher prices, and so increase margins and sell fewer policies;
- lower prices, and so reduce margins but sell more policies.

There are strategic and tactical reasons for insurers to increase or lower premiums.

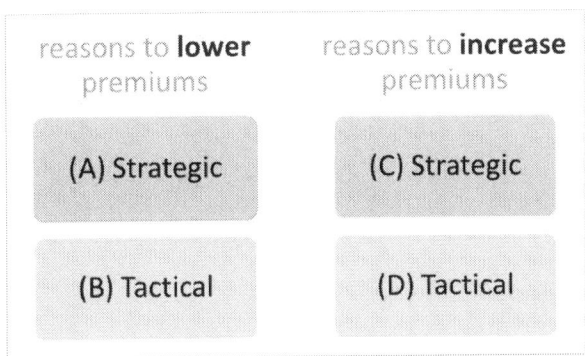

Figure 36: Reasons for increasing or lowering premiums

A) The main strategic reasons for the insurer to lower premiums are:

- to increase market share in the segments in which it wants to be more visible;
- to acquire knowledge and experience in a market, to decide whether this market is worth entering. The insurer invests, by reducing its profit margins, in order to learn more about operations in a market that it neither understands nor commands.

B) The main tactical reasons to lower premiums are:

- to discourage the entry of new competitors. Reducing the average premium may undermine returns from potential new comers.

- maximising short-term results. In the insurance business, the time lag between collecting the premium and the time when the insurer will bear the cost of claims made under the policy, significantly facilitates outstanding achievement in the short term. The consequence of an increase in revenue resulting from selling more insurance policies (although at lower prices) will only be felt at some time in the future when claims are made under such policies.

- gaining a customer by charging below average prices. This option may be justified:

    o if the overall business turnover compensates for a reduction in profits;

    o when the insurer needs a reference to change its image on the market;

    o if this business is a platform from which to attract other customers, which as a whole, means that average planned profits can be achieved.

- Increasing sales in another business. Sacrificing some margin of a product that is part of a business that contains other products of greater strategic importance is fairly frequent. Personal accident insurance or life insurance, because of their high profitability and low premiums, are often used in this type of tactic, enabling insurers to increase the sales turnover of insurance with a higher average premium, such as a comprehensive motor insurance.

C) The main strategic reasons for insurers to increase premiums are:

- To avoid the exit of inefficient competitors. Insurers with unsuitable cost structures only survive if the average premium level remains high enough to generate a margin to cover these costs. However, if the more inefficient insurers occupy positions that others do not want (whether customers, activities or geographical areas), it is in the interest of competitors to maintain these relative positions as it relieves them of doing business in areas that do not interest them or for which they have no vocation.

- Milking a business is justified, for example, when the competition is not particularly aggressive or when customer demands for it show signs of dormancy, providing the rate of contract cancellation is not a business weak point and price flexibility is a known and controlled variable.

Variations in premiums (in whatever sense) above a certain amount (approximately 5%), warns customers that there is a benefit in shopping around for competing proposals.

D) The main tactical reasons to increase premiums are:

- To avoid cannibalisation among different types of insurance. Marketing insurance below a certain level may justify cancelling other contracts the customer already has with the insurer and that meet the same needs, which is prejudicial if those other products generate higher profit margins for the insurer.

This situation occurs with pension and retirement schemes when they are sold at rates the same as other financial insurances or bank deposits. This can lead to cancelling these products and this heightens conflict between distribution channels.

However, cannibalisation can be positive for the insurer if the alternative is the loss of a customer to a competitor product.

- Increase medium term results. The increase of average premiums increases the solvency of the insurer. The sale of fewer policies, but at a higher price, leads to a reduction in competitive ability but creates a capital reserve that improves combined ratios.

In conclusion, there is justification for increasing or reducing insurance premiums. Either alternative can be a good choice, bringing positive results to the insurer. What is not advisable, however, are inconsistent changes not based on weighted decisions. The market does not understand, and consequently penalises, disjointed, erratic, irregular, unplanned moves. Not understanding the decisions of the insurer, customers, intermediaries and even employees, can no longer rely on the insurer and consequently on its proposals.

7B6) Positioning in a competitive environment

The price rate applied by the insurer determines the competitive environment in which it is positioned. The basic choice is to decide on whether to compete on price or on other factors (such as quality of service or innovative proposals).

Creaming the market or penetrating the market

The option to cream or penetrate the market is associated with the insurer's pricing policy and this has a direct effect on communication objectives.

In creaming the market, the insurer focuses on the distinguishing features of any insurance that is above its price. This option applies when products have competitive advantages over competitor proposals. These advantages may involve innovation, which is highly appreciated by customers, and generates higher profit margins. In these cases, communication policy must be based on distinguishing factors, making the price factor relatively less important.

Given the importance of the distribution channel in the customer's decision-making process, the use of creaming should be complemented by adding incentives to agents.

In the case of market penetration, the aim is to increase the sales volume, exploring the purchase decision-making factors of the insurance that are more commonly and widely used by most customers, such as price.

This approach is common in mature markets, with standardised products, in which no one competitor stands out clearly from the others, as often happens in the sale of the compulsory motor insurance or labour accidents.

Agents need to have less costly products in their portfolio to serve those customers who want them, as well as to prove to other customers that the higher price of other insurance is not due to competitive failure on the part of the distributor or insurer, but to its intrinsic quality.

<u>When to cream or to penetrate the market</u>

Creaming and penetration of the market may be more or less profitable. In both cases success requires the insurer to adjust its organisation, configuring all its processes coherently.

- If the insurer chooses to compete on the lower price market, it has to be structured as a low cost provider, developing simple, less customised products, selecting lower cost channels and communicating appropriately to reach those customers for whom price is the fundamental decision-making factor.

- If the insurer chooses not to compete on the basis of low prices, it must specialise in services to segments that favour factors other than low pricing, although the insurer must always present competitive prices for the quality it offers, developing skills in:

    o becoming aware of and attending to customers;

    o innovating products and processes to support its activity;

    o communicating its unique and distinct advantages;

    o training and preparing distributors, and equipping them with strong technical arguments to demonstrate that the difference in premiums is compensated by the increase in the benefits and advantages offered by the proposed insurance.

There is no scientific evidence to prove that those customers more sensitive to price are less loyal than others. In any case, in making their initial decision, customers are convinced that they have chosen the best available option, so that there is no motive strong enough for them to begin a new search for information on a product or process that, basically, does not engage them.

Similar to customers who make a price-based decision because they have found the cheapest product, customers that make their choice based on other criteria believe they have made the best choice within these criteria. Consequently, just as a new cheaper product may lead customers to rethink their decision, new products that seem better in the other criteria may lead customers to change their decision.

7C) Insurance distribution

The insurance intermediary is any individual or company that receives payment for conducting the business of insurance mediation.

Insurance mediation is the business of proposing an insurance contract or taking other preparatory steps to signing it, actually signing the insurance contract, or supporting the management and enforcement of the contract, namely the settlement of claims.

7C1) Description of insurance distribution channels

The main insurance distribution channels are divided into: direct, traditional and other business channels.

Figure 37: Distribution channels

Direct distribution channels

The direct sale is distinguished from other methods by the fact that there is no mediator between the insurer and the end customer. The two main direct sales categories are:

- the insurance office;
- remote sales, mainly phone and Internet channels.

The insurance office

Insurance offices are seeing sales turnover in insurance gradually falling because increasingly customers find them less attractive as a location in which to purchase insurance.

Insurance offices will continue to lose ground because they lack advantage when compared to other channels, both from the point of view of the customer and the insurer, given that they have fixed overheads, which in other distribution channels are converted into variable costs. In several developed countries the importance of the insurance office as a sales channel is already insignificant.

Some insurers with larger networks of their own offices have been converting them into back-up offices for the work of agents, and gradually eliminating their own function as direct sales outlets. The trend is for insurance offices to relocate out of city centres into areas that are quick and easy to access, now that they have repositioned themselves.

Phone

The phone was the first channel used for the remote sale of insurance, although it has never been particularly successful.

Currently its importance as a sales channel is decreasing. It has become increasingly restricted as a sales channel due to the support provided by other distribution channels, including the Internet.

However, the phone channel has gained some importance in using insurer data bases in projects involving customer retention and cross-selling, by identifying potential customers for business in other channels.

Internet

The Internet has high growth rates in most developed countries. Although not as significant as most direct insurer business plans had estimated, there is no doubt of its importance in providing a service to ever more customer segments.

This channel has become very important for providing information on brands and insurance.

The prediction is that this channel will become increasingly important, due to the ease, speed and cost of carrying out operations.

Traditional channels

Traditional intermediaries include agents that aim to reconcile the interests of customers with those of insurers, and brokers, who undertake essentially to protect the interests of their customers.

Agent

The insurance agent mediates on behalf of one or more insurance companies, under the terms of the contract held with any of these companies, and may receive premiums or amounts to be paid to policy-holders, insured persons or beneficiaries.

Remuneration is based on a commission on insurance sold and on incentives for achieving targets for growth and profitability.

Premiums paid to insurance agents are always considered as having been paid to the insurer, and sums delivered by the insurance company to the agent are only considered as having been paid to the policy-holder, insured person or beneficiary, once they have received these sums.

The role of insurance agents is of great importance to customers. The reason in many countries that they remain the customers' preferred distribution channel when purchasing non-life insurance products, despite the significant legal, regulatory, economic, social, political and technological changes that have reshaped the way in which this business operates, is recognition of their irreplaceable worth in providing support and advice, in the pre and post-sale of insurance contracts.

It is unlikely that agents will return to a position of dominance in the distribution of life insurance as there is no plan to add benefits that would justify a significant change in customer preference, that is, and comparing with the banking channel, in terms of an image of reliability and trust, costs, customer-friendly operations and speed.

Broker

Brokers have superior technical and administrative abilities, and form the channel best adapted to intermediation and management of risks that are more complex, sophisticated and large scale. Brokers also provide risk management consultancy and issue technical reports. They must operate their business for more than one insurance company so that they can always present more than one proposal to their customers.

Remuneration is based on a direct insurance commission and on case-based agreements, i.e., on the profitability of the business they mediate.

Bank

In many markets, banks are the preferred distribution channel for the sale of life insurance. This preference is due to the fact that banking networks are very much geared to selling insurance with a strong financial component and to binding the sale of risk products (whether life or non-life insurance) to bank loans. The trust that customers have in banks also determines their preference for purchasing financial life products and pension plans from them.

They normally act as tied agents, although they may take on other characteristics.

Other business channels

Companies from different sectors have been adapting its distribution networks to insurance distribution. Here are some examples.

Post office

This channel is geared mainly to the sale of very simple products (such as financial insurance) for middle and lower class customers more challenged culturally and with limited financial literacy, this being the profile of customers that:

- visit the post office more frequently;

- establish closer and trusting relationships with the respective employees;

- have time available to deal with several procedures available at post offices;

- have fewer customer alternatives as they are not the prime target of other channels, such as banks, and they are very familiar with the more technological channels.

Post office employees do not have the training, skills or vocation to sell complex and sophisticated insurance products and that alone determines the business that this channel can mediate.

Retail networks

Legislative changes affecting insurance mediation have opened up the possibility for other businesses to diversify into the distribution of insurance.

Commercial networks can be made more profitable, taking advantage of the power of respective brands (*brand assurance*). Some sectors where this type of diversification has been seen are in:

- retail stores;
- motor trade;
- armourers and gunsmiths;
- travel agencies;
- customer credit companies.

The UK market is generally presented as a successful example in this spread of insurance distribution channels. In Asia (namely in Southern China, India, Malaysia and the Philippines), there are a few examples of *mall-assurance*, but the development potential is high. *Mall-assurance* is the sale of insurance in large shopping malls that are visited daily by thousands of people. Two approaches are adopted:

- the availability of pre-formatted, integrated insurance solutions, for sale in shops and kiosks. These solutions are based on sets of cover, with few choices on offer and at a fixed price;

- the sale of insurance at very low prices by specialised promoters and the use of which can be easily identified by customers, usually personal accident or life. The aim of these sales is to get data on potential customers to be able to sell them other more complex products. A telephone call is made at a later date with the aim of selling additional insurance or scheduling a personal business meeting.

These insurance distribution models bring consistently good results, providing the customer's profile, market maturity and the legal framework meet the right conditions.

7C2) The exceptional importance of distribution in insurance

There are aspects of the insurance business that reveal the importance of distribution compared to other sectors of activity. This marketing variable must be managed carefully for a number of reasons, in particular:

- its historical and cultural importance. For many years, the insurance business has turned to external distribution networks for its growth, above all, in Europe, to the banking channel for life insurance and to agents and brokers for non-life insurance.

  With the exception of the Internet, the importance of which for insurance distribution is still low but growing, distribution structure is not expected to change in the near future, in view of the way in which most customers buy their insurance based on contacts with friends, family and acquaintances that work with or know people connected to banks and insurance companies.

- Minimum involvement of customers in the purchase process. Although basically customers recognise that insurance is important for safeguarding their personal well-being and property, they also recognise that it is unlikely a claim will occur or that they will face difficulties over claim settlements, and they also realise that purchasing insurance is a fairly unemotional operation.

  Consequently, the customer does not get involved in the insurance buying procedure, in most cases opting to delegate this decision to the mediator, agent, bank, broker or some other entity, even if there is a cost for such a service.

- The influence of distribution on other tactical variables. Although all marketing components influence one another, distribution has a particular effect on other variables in this business. The decision on which distribution channel to choose determines the insurer's other tactical options, as shown in figure 38, and has an effect on:

    o price policy;

    o product configuration;

    o communication model.

Channel	Product	Price	Communication
Agents, brokers	Diverse and varied (from very simple to very complex and sophisticated)	Medium and High	Making the most of the role of the agent (pull) and the competitive advantages of the insurer (push)
Bank	Diverse but simple	Medium and High	Focus on integrated financial solutions (cross-selling opportunities) and the soundness of the institutions involved
Phone, Internet	Limited offer, simple and compact	Low	Focus on the end customer, on price, speed and simplicity of processes

Figure 38: Effect of distribution channel on other marketing variables

Complex products can be distributed via the agent and broker channel, with a wide range of prices and communication that highlights the importance of pre-sale, sale and post-sale advice and monitoring.

The banking channel has neither the knowledge nor the technical skills required to sell more sophisticated insurance products, although it may have a wide range of cover and capital on offer. Also the banking channel can charge a price compatible with this range of cover on offer, facilitated by providing personalised support and communications that focus on complete financial solutions and the soundness of the channel.

In choosing the Internet channel, products and processes (at all levels of interaction with the customer) must be very simple and intuitive (meaning the specialist mediator can be removed), with very competitive prices because:

- customers expect, at least, to avoid brokerage charges;

- brands can be compared easily, which increases aggression between competing proposals;

- there is mass communication and a target market, because a preference for simple, inexpensive products is found throughout all social classes and types of company.

The opposite situation, in which other tactical marketing variables affect the choice of distribution channel, is not as significant and decisive. If, for instance, the insurer positions itself in the lower price segment, these products can be placed in any distribution channel.

• Long-term commitments involved, to the extent that to be in any distribution channel, there is a very significant level of internal skills, employee training, process development and technological investment required (throughout all insurance company activities).

The choice of a particular distribution channel entails forming external partnerships. In the case of mediation, many agreements, with many agents, covering many characteristics and objectives, are necessary.

Fewer agreements are required in the case of brokers, and there is less diversity than there is with agents, but the insurer is much more dependent on fewer distributors, not really an advisable situation.

In the case of a bank, usually only one agreement is established, but of long duration and with much greater depth and sophistication than agreements established with other channels.

Channel	Number of partnership agreements	Duration of agreements	Complexity of agreements / depth of relationship
Agents	***	*	*
Brokers	**	**	**
Banks	*	***	***

Figure 39: Impact of partnership agreements with agents, brokers and banks

The new distribution channels, that is, phone and Internet, demand a considerable investment in technology.

On the other hand, the cost of maintaining commercial outlets should always be taken into consideration in all models that use them, even when they are still relevant and the sales option is to use these traditional channels.

Contrary to the idea that, once eliminated, insurance mediation services will never return again as new direct distribution channels develop, particularly the Internet, it seems that the role of the agent is still highly valued, above all for insurance contracts that are more complex and/or of greater value.

The agent's role is far more comprehensive than a simple sales channel and involves the management of customer risks. But agents must not focus their arguments on the price of insurance, otherwise their range of action will be limited to selling very simple products that can be purchased more easily through direct channels.

When customers can purchase and manage their contracts through direct channels the advisory role of the agent will become more important than that of simply making a sale. As the whole process evolves the way in which intermediaries are remunerated will change from a commission on sales to the payment of a retainer for customer risk management. Customers will determine how much they are willing to pay for having a certain degree of cover for their main risks, leaving it to the agent to manage this fund in the most effective way for the customer, and this will include the agent's own fee.

Agents have to be experts in their role. The ability to diagnose the customer's major risks and to mitigate and cover them is a task that is increasingly more important and complex, given that:

- risks are more complex;
- alternatives are more diverse;
- the amount of information available is increasing;
- there are more variables to consider in the decision-making process;
- the time that customers have available to devote to tasks outside their professional or family life is becoming increasingly scarce.

Agents need to move towards understanding the private and professional particulars of their customers, and for this they need solid technical skills, the ability to master analytical tools and to use new communication resources, in particular the social media.

Their success depends increasingly on their ability to create value for customers, that value consisting of finding the best insurance solutions, compatible with customer idiosyncrasies, and solutions that will protect them at the best price from personal and property risks that threaten them severely and frequently.

Optimization of complementary channels

There are many benefits to be gained for agents who cooperate with one another, rather than destroying value and cannibalising business from one another. There are business deals that are blocked because a certain channel inhibits the progress of another, bringing a loss for all involved, including customers. Insurers gain from promoting integrated distribution channels so as to optimise value for customers.

The following are examples of specific initiatives that insurers should promote:

- Taking advantage of contacts received or generated in the insurance company (for example, by phone or email), with a view to selling new products, retaining customers that seem ready to break ties with the insurer, or to win back customers that have left. These opportunities must be forwarded to the points of sale (internal or agent). The insurer should develop calculation procedures that indicate precisely which entity is best suited to managing these customers effectively. The following variables should be included in this calculation:

    o Geographical proximity to the customer;

    o Claims rate of the agent;

    o Average customer value;

    o Average stay time of customers with the distributor.

    Should minimum levels of average customer value or retention levels not be achieved, the agent's priority in allocating new business opportunities must be significantly reduced.

- Cases where, for regulatory reasons or others, the distributor (possibly an agent, a broker or a bank) cannot manage its customers, they must be transferred to the insurance company to ensure their management continues, after which they may be returned to the original distributor, or if that is not possible, then to another mediator, using the procedure described in the previous paragraph.

- Should a customer require a more complex product from a channel (such as a bank or the internet) that does not sell this type of product, a specialist distributor, recommended by the insurer, can handle this requirement to ensure the business is not lost.

- Agreements established between distributors with complementary interests. There are cases of entities having difficulty in maintaining their business because of competition, and with the resources and determination to expand. The insurer may have a decisive role in getting these entities with complementary interests to:

    o meet, get to know one another and negotiate;

    o establish conditions in which a partnership can be formed to generate benefits for both parties;

    o have the logistic, bureaucratic and administrative conditions available for their association to be profitable.

Insurers should make the most of synergies between channels demonstrating how the multi-channel option contributes to strengthening the insurer, its channels and an improvement in customer satisfaction. The challenge for insurers is to select the best combination of communication channels, distribution channels and access modes (in person, phone, Internet, etc.) for each customer. Progressing to multi-access means that new business models must be designed, in which online and offline contacts coexist and prove their worth.

Multi-access combines the convenience of remote access, with face-to-face tailored advice. It is customers who decide, at any time, on how they wish to contact the insurer. In relating to the customer, multi-access clearly improves services and increases interaction because there is a platform that provides all contacts (via the Internet, phone and through person-to-person networks).

From experience in applying this model, the phenomenon of channel cannibalisation was reduced. The net effect of the multi-channel concept for traditional insurers is clearly positive because it attracts new customer segments.

The insurance company's business model, in regard to its distribution channels, must take into consideration:

- that each customer segment has its preferred method of interacting with the insurer. This method has to be understood in order to suit the operating model and to achieve the desired level of service and results;

- channels in which the insurer should invest, based on a matrix determining how attractive each insurance is to each channel, taking into consideration geographical area, customer segment and types of product, and to use this matrix in dealing with multi-channel issues, such as overlapping or conflict.

Integrating distribution channels benefits all parties involved in the insurance business, namely customers, agents and the insurer itself.

A) The main customer benefits are:

- increased flexibility and easy access, which makes the insurer permanently available;

- assurance that personal attention is available (the agent or the actual insurer at its branch offices);

- an increase in the range of purchase options.

B) From the agent's perspective, the main benefits are:

- access to new customer segments that began their insurance purchasing process through other channels and who have been passed on to the agent;

- possibility of earning from business done by its customers in other channels or from the provision of services;

- the chance for cross-selling to customers that did not deal with the agent initially;

- releasing time spent on tasks that add little value, and which the customer can deal with through other channels, faster and more conveniently.

C) From an insurer's perspective, the main benefits are:

- broadening the scope of its business geographically, and being present in places where it does not have a physical network;

- access to new customer segments;

- increasing profit margins in being able to define a commission policy based on the performance of each distribution channel;

- increasing efficiency, by enabling customer queries and complaints to be clarified and resolved, before they become major issues.

In conclusion, customers adopt behaviour that is increasingly hybrid in their relationship with insurers, turning to the different channels in order to meet different types of need. The multi-channel approach is an increasingly more indispensable response for insurers to this pattern of behaviour, economic impact of which has to be monitored, namely:

- the increase in revenue from entering new customer segments, greater retention and an increase in the value of each customer through additional cross-selling. However, the possibility of having to make discounts on purchases made by current customers in new channels, can contribute to a fall in revenue;

- increase of costs, as a result of the necessary investments in:
    - people, such as call centres and information systems;

- o   new communication and information technologies;

- o   marketing, directed at distribution channels and customers;

- Cost reductions come mainly through synergies gained from the better use of resources in business support operations.

7C3) Creating value for intermediaries

Value can be created for agents by increasing benefits or reducing costs. Both can be based on monetary or non-monetary components.

<u>Monetary Benefits</u>

Monetary benefits may vary in nature (which is found in most cases), or fixed. The main monetary benefits are:

- commissions, usually based on a percentage of the premiums agents charge customers. This percentage varies with the strategic importance and the profits to be made from each insurance line and cover.

  It is common, for example, for a commission of 10% to be paid on commercial premiums charged for home insurance, in all cover provided, except for seismic risk where no commission is usually paid, given the low profits the insurer makes on this type of cover due to the high cost of reinsurance.

  In addition to commission on sales, there are also commissions on collection, paid to agents that have collection approval, and brokerage, inherent in the status of insurance broker.

  Efforts made by many insurers to increase direct debit payments has led to the out-moded, but understandable, situation in which agents are paid a collection commission, not for collecting insurance premiums, but based on the agent's ability to encourage customers to accept this payment method.

In certain conditions, exceptional commissions may be paid. The purpose of this is to gain the accounts and the loyalty of agents who are particularly important to the insurer for several reasons, such as:

- their above average business turnover;

- their geographical importance enables the insurer to establish itself in a given region.

* kick-back means paying agents an agreed sum in proportion to the objectives they achieve. These agreements are usually negotiated and signed between the months of October and December of the previous year. During the year, the insurance company keeps agents informed on changes to the variables negotiated and the forecast value of their *kick-back*. This allows agents to monitor business developments and, if necessary, introduce corrective measures at the appropriate time. At the end of the year the extent to which objectives have been achieved, and the corresponding *kick-back amounts*, are determined.

* payment of specific compensation for fulfilling certain objectives, within a given period of time and in a certain geographical area. These objectives, for example, may consist of:

    - increasing the market shares of a product;

    - obtaining profiles or contact data on customers;

    - reducing the rate of customer abandonment;

    - not exceeding a certain level of claims.

* payment for carrying out certain bureaucratic or administrative tasks. The success of decentralising, and assigning tasks traditionally conducted by insurance companies to agents, means that agents are paid a fee for carrying out these operations. This does not diminish

the importance of some of these tasks to customers because of their speed and quality of services provided;

- the payment of a fixed monthly fee is particularly applicable when agents first open their business as it enables them to cope with start-up costs. This type of benefit may cover the rent on their commercial space, computer equipment, furniture, car purchase or payment to an employee. In return, agents usually remain as the insurer's exclusive distributors for a given period of time.

Paying variable monetary benefits based on meeting the insurer's objectives is generally better for the insurer than fixed benefits, in that:

- they are more stimulating and motivating, both for agents who are challenged to win, and for the insurer who can also set objectives for its internal commercial structures;

- disputes with agents are less likely because paying benefits without off-setting them might suggest that one party benefits unfairly.

Non-monetary Benefits

Non-monetary benefits are very important because they relate to the agent's speed, simplicity, flexibility and cost. In addition, the relational component is increasingly more important, particularly in experiences that strengthen the emotional connection between the agent and the insurer and the latter's employees.

Intermediaries agents often choose insurers for two main characteristics:

- they are competitive, because, as a rule, the key factor is not to be the cheapest, as this would lower agent commissions, but more competitive in the price/cover provided in an insurance. At a certain level, no matter how much the insurance is worth, price puts the agent outside the range of choice for potential customers;

- the ease and speed with which issues are resolved, both in pre-sale (when, for example, the speed and simplicity of the premium simulation platform is fundamental), sale, and post-sale, above all providing information and dealing with claim settlement procedures.

Insurers must implement the risk control measures endorsed by their agents, without increasing bureaucracy.

Just as important as the price factor for an agent selecting an insurer, is the speed and simplicity with which operations are carried out. Besides benchmarking price competitiveness on a regular basis, insurers should also do comparative studies on the speed and simplicity with which processes on its platforms are implemented.

The most common non-monetary benefits are:

- The availability of information and communication systems. This is one of the most important benefits to agents, because these systems enable agents to work faster and more effectively, and these are two of the most important critical success factors in insurance mediation.

    Insurers must have a system that allows agents to manage their customers, claims, policies and receipts, simply. Financial processes, particularly clearing accounts with the insurer, should be streamlined.

    An agent needs to access information for monitoring its business in real time, given the importance of speed to its success in gaining new business and for retaining current business.

    Alert and message systems pointing to business opportunities or potential loss of customers are increasingly appreciated by agents.

    Some examples of the main impact of their use are:

    - a significant reduction in bureaucratic and administrative tasks, at no cost to the intermediary or to the customer;

- a dramatic reduction in costs related to transport, equipment and supplies;

- improvement in the quality of service provided to customers, providing them with information and inaccurate data;

- an increase in sales to existing customers. There is often great concern in attracting new customers when there is a large potential for selling new products, more cover or an increase of sums insured to current customers;

- The experiences provided. Insurer proposals tend to be much the same so that relationships with the insurer's employees are decisive in attracting agents and their loyalty. Public relations events, such as business conventions and trips away with agents, are examples of relevant tactics offered to agents;

- Equipment, namely computer and telecommunications equipment;

- Property, namely the lease and acquisition of spaces for installing commercial agencies for agents. The office materials and furniture required for operating an insurance sales office are often included under this heading;

- Promoting the agent through local communication campaigns, paid for or reimbursed by the insurer, business cards, signs, merchandising material and, increasingly, websites;

- Training and information. Training should focus on technical issues, management processes and business management. Meetings to review national and regional insurance markets are also highly valued. These components are very important to agents because what differentiates them is their knowledge and competence in giving advice and solving the problems of their customers.

7C4) Conflicts between distribution channels

The multi-distribution model, based on the use of several different distribution channels by the same insurer, is the one best suited to of the demands of most customers. Each insurance-channel has advantages and disadvantages for customers, so that optimising their purchasing procedure includes exploring the benefits each channel has to offer for each type of product. Customers can, for example (merely by way of figure):

- purchase their health insurance through an agent, with the advantage of duly understanding how the insurance operates, the medical networks and the associated bureaucratic procedures.

- purchase a third party liability environmental insurance for their industry from a broker because of his independent, technical advice;

- a construction insurance through a broker because he can offer technical, independent advice;

- acquire a pension and retirement plan at a bank, given the diversity of options available and the efficiency with which the purchase is made;

- buy motor insurance over the Internet, because the price is lower and the process fast and simple.

Conflicts between channels caused by multi-distribution must not limit channel development. Different types of conflict must be identified and adequately managed. These conflicts are caused because insurers distribute their insurance through different distribution channels and they make agreements with distributors who, within the same type of channel, have very different characteristics and objectives.

The main conflicts between channels

The main types of conflict between distribution channels occur for the following reasons:

- breach of rules;

- different objectives;

- lack of definition in relationship rules.

Breach of operating rules

All insurers have their rules and procedures for conducting business and claims settlement.

The fiduciary responsibility of insurers demands that operations be strictly controlled and audited. However, these procedures can reduce the ease, speed and simplicity with which their agents do business.

The insurer should carefully consider and monitor all its decisions on this subject. After defining its procedures, it should implement them strictly, because when agents fail to comply with the rules stipulated for the business, they may gain an unfair competitive advantage over those agents who do comply with them. Those who do not comply, for example, may be in a position to attract business that those failing to comply cannot achieve.

This is always a latent conflict that the insurer has to prevent because of the risks it would cause to the insurer's very existence.

Difference in objectives

The distribution networks of traditional insurers include agents with different objectives and ways of operating.

There are, for example, agents or banks that, in becoming established in a certain region, implement aggressive business plans in order to achieve high growth rates in the short-term, although, temporarily, they have to forego part of their profit margin. Other agents or banks, with substantial insurance portfolios, and that have reached a certain degree of stability, may aim to maximise the income they earn from their existing customers, as it is in their interests to prevent prices from falling.

If agents in these two scenarios are within the same strategic range of action (in other words, at a distance close enough for customers to *shop around*), it is inevitable that conflicts will arise from different objectives and the disparity of business models.

A lack of definition in relationship rules

These conflicts arise because the insurer perceives there is a situation of competitive disloyalty in a certain channel because insurance has been placed in alternative channels at a lower price.

This frequently causes conflict between the agent and Internet channels. Although recognising that the price of insurance can vary when brokerage commissions are not applied, Internet growth comes partially at the expense of the agents' business.

From the perspective of the insurer, the solution involves developing the business in the different channels, but entirely openly and transparently, creating different value proposals with separate products, prices and communications for the different channels. It is particularly important to define the criteria by which each channel can claim possession of each business deal and each customer, as well as the conditions in which business and customers can be transferred between channels.

There are also insurance companies that distribute their products exclusively through banking channels because:

- they are positioned, organised, structured and configured to serve a banking network;

- the partner (bank) imposes its negotiating power demanding exclusive distribution of that particular brand of insurance.

Managing channel conflicts

Conflicts between distribution channels should be avoided and not allowed to get out of hand. In certain cases they may be unavoidable, but the extent of their impact can be controlled.

The fundamental principles of conflict prevention and control between channels are the following:

- establishing clear rules for relationships between all parties;
- monitoring the daily routine of agents (at least the most important ones) closely and attentively;
- communicating smoothly, openly, transparently and systematically with channels;
- encouraging synergies between channels.

Establishing clear rules for relationships between all parties

There can be no doubts, ambiguities or lack of definition in this field. All agents must know the rules on how to relate to the insurer and to other agents, as well as the conditions in which each business can be conducted.

Monitoring the daily routine of agents closely and attentively

Close monitoring of agents helps detect problems right from the start of problem symptoms arising. The early detection of signs of disagreement is the only way to resolve them before they reach critical levels.

Communicating smoothly, openly, transparently and systematically with channels

A lack of information leads to speculation, uncertainty, rumours and suspicion. Any decisions affecting the insurer as a whole and marketing in particular must be shared with the distribution network so that it has access to information originating with the insurer. The insurer's employees must be prepared, trained and informed so that they can clear up any doubts, questions and uncertainties raised by the distribution network and by customers, quickly and with due explanation.

Maximising synergies between channels

The insurer should share the benefits derived from being in multiple channels with distribution channels, as indicated in the examples under the heading "The exceptional importance of distribution in insurance".

7D) Communication in insurance

Communication is each and every sign that the insurer sends to the market and the entities with which it relates. All moments of contact, all interactions undertaken by the insurer, its employees, distributors or shareholders, contribute to forming favourable or unfavourable perceptions of the insurer.

The insurers' models of communication have been radically altered by two main factors:

- technological developments;
- the rise in importance of the social media.

It is essential to monitor interactions occurring regularly with the surrounding community.

7D1) Central aspects in defining communication policy

In defining the insurer's communication policy, the following questions have to be considered and planned:

- the communication objective, with a view to the desired effect;
- to whom it is intended, i.e. the recipients of the communication;

- definition of the most appropriate message to achieve planned objectives;

- how to disseminate the message, considering the means to be used;

- when to communicate, establishing the most appropriate moment.

<u>The desired effect</u>

Brands need to communicate to be relevant, in order to:

- draw attention.

    One of the basic operations of the brand is to ensure the reputation of the insurer and its proposals, which is particularly important:

    - in commercial dynamics, impacting the brand's ability to identify and attract business;

    - in the tolerance of the different target groups to any possible misunderstandings, errors and omissions;

    - in gaining and retaining good customers, agents and employees.

    Equally important is the management of the insurer's institutional image.

    The way in which the insurer communicates is also very important to ensure that political, legal and regulatory forces do not obstruct its business. This effect of communication is different in not aiming to meet immediate business goals.

- educate, revealing new information, highlighting its importance or the consequences of not using it.

- The insurer must always be concerned with improving the user experience. The insurer should disclose regularly the value that it creates for its customers and distribution channels, both in absolute terms, by highlighting benefits provided, and in relative terms, by comparing it to the value proposals made by its main competitors.

- persuade, with the purpose of encouraging the desired customer behaviour.

    When the effect is to increase sales, the following are some possible outcomes:

    o customer awareness of the need for insurance;

    o creating interest in a practical solution;

    o placing the brand among the customers preferred alternatives;

    o enhancing its strengths or strengthening the perception of benefits the insurance offers;

    o maintaining customer satisfaction.

The targets of communication

The initial step is to identify the targets of communication, which then determines the following stages in the process. The individuals or companies targeted by the communication can vary widely:

- customers, in all dimensions, including:

    o policy-holders;

    o new and current customers that have recently acquired a new insurance, new coverage or increased the sums insured by its policies;

    o customers that have cancelled their contracts, reduced the scope of coverage, increased the deductible or that have reduced the policy sums insured;

- o   potential customers who are entities that require insurance and, although in a position to purchase it, have not done so;

- o   individuals insured (that may not be the policy-holder);

- o   beneficiaries of a policy who, in the case of life-insurance, may be the legal heirs, or the mortgage lenders in contracts linked to bank loans;

- o   customers from competitors that already have insurance with other insurers;

- decision makers and those that influence;

- agents, whether exclusive to the insurer or not;

- employees, in their different roles, responsibilities and profiles, as well as their representatives;

- institutional entities, namely regulatory and supervisory bodies, other insurers, sector-based associations (insurance agents and brokers), trade unions and customer protection bodies;

- the local community and the public in general.

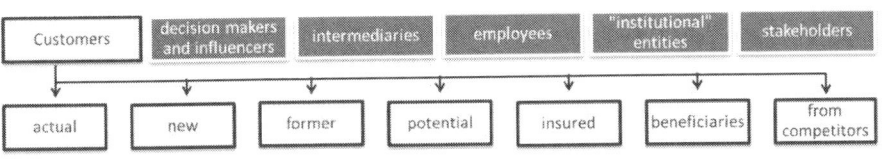

Figure 40: Communication targets

Communication skills must be developed for each of these groups. Knowing how to communicate is often wrongly confused with the oral or written power of speech. The key is to understand the target audience being addressed in the communication, as well as its specific characteristics and the possibility of establishing and maintaining valuable interactions.

The communication message

If the insurer wishes to achieve business goals through communication, the insurance purchasing and decision-making processes must be understood, particularly the following factors:

- rational factors, relating to how the customer acquires the insurance and the benefits it gains from it;

- emotional factors, which relate to how the customer feels in purchasing and using the insurance, in particular, how it affects the customer's customs, habits and behaviour in the many aspects of the customer's life (personal, family, social and professional).

If the effects are of another nature, maximum accuracy, reasoning, assertiveness and objectivity in communications must be ensured.

Means of communication

As with other communication variables, the means depend on the insurer's strategy and are interdependent on other marketing variables.

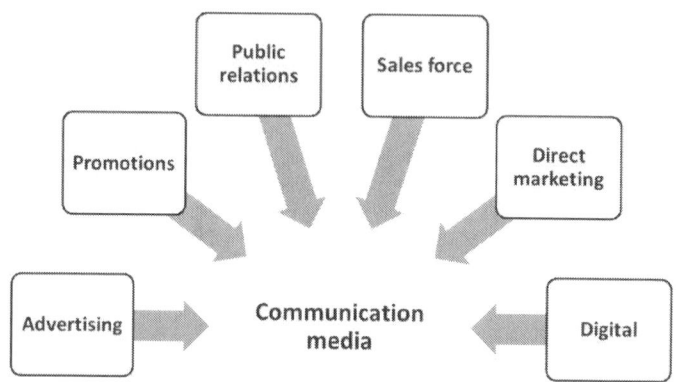

Figure 41: Means of communication

Advertising

This covers forms of paid communication, not geared to specific individuals but to groups of customers, examples being:

- the more conventional means, geared to mass customers (individuals and companies), such as television, press and radio;

- merchandising, such as posters, leaflets and brochures, among others, are also forms of advertising.

- symbols that embody the brand, its values and positioning, such as the logo, the colours, the signature or the jingle.

Colours have a very important role to play in how insurance is perceived by customers. Their meaning is influenced by the cultural references of each region. Most insurers adopt one of the following colours:

   o blue, for example for Allianz, Axa, Liberty, Macif and Zurich;

   o green in the case of Groupama;

   o red for Generali and Mapfre.

The choice of colour reveals how the insurer is positioned and how it wants to be perceived. Even if adopting a certain colour or a certain logo only considers aesthetic factors, all the implications of this choice must be borne in mind.

Each colour has positive connotations that correspond to the values the insurer should be associated with, and negative ones, that it must reduce, as indicated in figure 42.

Colour	Positive associations	Negative associations	Use
Red	Dynamic approach and pro-activity	War, blood and fire	- Minimalist, as a way of drawing attention to detail; - Image of power and passion.
Orange	Activity, generosity and ambition	Discredit and lack of consideration	- Friendly, close environment; - Image of movement and energy.
Yellow	Joy and expansiveness	Cowardice and doubt	- Environment of happiness.
Green	Security, satisfaction and rest	Aggressive (bluish) and unhealthy (greyish)	- Environment of balance and harmony.
Blue	Justice, seriousness and tranquillity	Secret and shadow	- Appropriate for enterprising environments; - The lighter shades are suitable for the social media.
Violet	Nobility, abundance, dignity and imagination	Mystery and oppression	- Select and distinct environments, with luxury and wealth. - The lighter shades are associated with romance.
Black	Distinction, discipline and power	Despair and ignorance	- Environments of elegance and modernity.
White	Perfection, truth and wisdom	Emptiness and silence	- Environment of simplicity, openness and cleanliness.

Figure 42: Positive and negative associations of different colours

Promotions

Promotions are incentives that improve sales and retain business and customers, and they are attributed to distribution channels or directly to end customers.

This form of communication is very important in the insurance industry, and is one of the main elements in commercial development plans, due to:

- the importance of monetary incentives to create and keep a distribution channel active, effective and loyal;

- the difficulty in differentiating between Insurance companies and their offers, in a way sufficiently valued by customers.

Public Relations

Public relations consist of initiatives adopted by employees, managers, and even the shareholders of the insurance company, or their representatives, such as communication agencies or lawyers, and that aim to enhance the image of the insurer and strengthen relations with local entities. Public relations can be approached in several ways, such as:

- local, regional, national or international commercial conventions;
- road shows;
- seminars, workshops and symposiums;
- annual trips designed to reward those distributors who are more successful, or the insurer's most valued customers.

Sales Force

The insurer's sales force involves its employees with the roles of:

- representing the insurer with intermediaries and end customers, with the aim of developing profitable growth for the business;
- direct sales, although in several developed countries this approach is becoming less relevant.

Insurers have a responsibility to guarantee that their employees are trained and motivated in order to carry out their role successfully, particularly in technical, commercial and behavioural terms. The insurer's market image and the results of distribution channels depend on this training and motivation.

Direct marketing

Direct marketing encompasses one-to-one interactions between the insurer and a certain entity, who may be a customer, a partner or a supplier.

Although this is very effective and avoids the waste inherent in other forms of mass address, there are two constraints, which although decreasing, do hold back the development of this form in the insurance sector:

- less priority given to direct contact between the insurer and its customers as a result of the number of agents intervening, in the developed countries, in the distribution of non-life products, and bank intervention in life insurance;

- poor quality data available on customers in the information systems of many insurers.

  Attempts to overcome this limitation by offering incentives for the collection of customer data have not proved effective in the medium term. Although these initiatives do generate some response (around 10% of contacts are highly positive), a significant part of this data is out-of-date by the following year. Insurers need to implement processes for on-going improvement, such as increasing the frequency of customer contacts and with every contact check and complete customer data.

The excessive number of irrelevant messages targeted at customers can also limit the development of this communication medium. Insurers need to assess the interest and relevance of all their communications. Customers clearly distinguish between contacts that have content of interest to them. However, there are many more communication failures by default, due to insurers communicating less than they should, rather than communicating too much.

This means of communication is gradually becoming more important in the insurance sector given its advantages compared to alternatives. However, this requires developing skills in areas such as:

- information technology systems, particularly the creation, management and maintenance of the customer databases;

- communications, taking into account the need to develop content that is relevant and objective, adapted to these means and with the regularity and format appropriate to each recipient.

Digital Media

Digital media are the most recent and fastest growing means of communication. The methods used by customers to obtain information and entertainment, as well as how they perceive and become involved with brands, are changing irrevocably. One effect of the emergence of the digital media has had is on the revolutionary segmentation and fragmentation of markets compared to conventional means of communication.

The change in how we communicate has evolved in such a way as to:

- increase investment and focus the attention of corporate decision-makers on these means of communication;
- develop different formats that promote interactions with the public. The information obtained by bi-directional communication is very useful for the insurer to establish its priorities, making the information from these means of communication fundamental because of its importance to marketing;
- create new metrics to measure the effectiveness and the return on investments made in communications;
- integrate digital advertising with traditional methods;
- develop new skills and abilities to deal with new means of information and communication.

Although, in general, insurance company budgets for communications and publicity are not increasing, there is a significant rise in investment in the digital media (such as cable television, mobile devices, video games and the Internet), which suggests less being used for other means of communication.

This trend is the result of a combination of several factors:

- the constant increase in the price of traditional means of communication, aggravated by the fact it is becoming less effective.

The new media helps dramatically reduce the cost of producing and distributing campaigns, and also introduces constant and instant improvements to messages while campaigns are underway;

- changes in customer behaviour reflected, for example, in new expectations from advertising;
- the use of digital means eliminates the gap between the time that the message is sent and the desired customer reaction (such as obtaining information or buying an insurance), given that this response takes no more than a click.

Despite the natural inertia of communication departments in insurance companies, institutional and culturally accustomed to slow-moving traditional methods used in their planning, digital media is gaining ground. This trend will increase as communication departments become familiar with digital environments.

7D2) Pushing the offer (*push*), or pulling the offer (*pull*)

Business communication can be steered as a priority to the distribution channel or the end customer.

With the option to push the insurance, communication concentrates on the distribution channel. Agents are encouraged to sell insurance by receiving incentives, benefits, commissions or bonuses on additional sales.

This is the most commonly used option in the insurance sector because customers are scarcely involved with insurance companies and in the purchase process, which also explains the importance of the distribution channel in this business.

The alternative is to pull the insurance by focusing communication on the end customer, increasing the sales from customer requests and demands on distribution channels.

This is the model indicated in the following cases:

- in direct business models, namely in cases of sales made via Internet or phone;

- when customers perceive differences between available brands, which is relatively more frequent with business customers, who attach more to innovation, or who need to cover more complex and sophisticated risks;

- if there is a relevant set of customers that are loyal to a brand, which can be seen in the aforementioned cases (chapter 3B - Nominal choices made through customer loyalty).

7E) Complementary variables of the insurance marketing-mix

The marketing-mix is a concept initially developed for products (not for the services), focused on North American industrial sectors. In its adaptation to services, inadequacies were identified due to overlooking some key elements in its definition: physical evidence, processes and, most importantly, people.

In essence, a service is a process carried out by people in a particular physical environment.

7E1) Physical evidence

Physical evidence is a variable that is crucial to the insurance business because of the importance of replacement indicators for the purchase decision. Physical aspects materialise according to the way the insurer positions itself, consequently inferring its strengths and weaknesses. For this reason physical evidence must be managed with great care, particularly:

- the appearance of its offices;

- its headquarters;

- documents given to customers;

- advertising campaigns;
- websites.

7E2) Processes

Processes unite the services provided. In the insurance business, the processes associated with claim settlement are particularly important because customers acquire a guarantee that if a random event identified in the policy occurs, the insurer will reimburse them for their losses, quickly and simply. However, most customers will never make a claim, so the quality assessment of the insurance and insurer will be based on interactions established with agents or websites.

All processes must be designed and, periodically, analysed, assessed and audited, for their simplicity, speed, and cost to the insurer and to other entities with whom it relates. The more visible, documented and certified the processes are, the better the insurer will be able to manage and control them, in order to convert these processes into competitive advantages or, at least, avoid their becoming *bottlenecks*.

There are insurers that position themselves according to the advantages conferred by their processes, such as, those positioned as being easiest and fastest in selling their insurance and in claim management.

7E3) People

The people are a determining factor in differentiating among insurers, and that affects all other positioning factors.

The trust, diversity and inevitability of insurance, in addition to the difficulty in innovating solutions and processes, reveal the importance of people to the success of this business.

Managing people is one of the most important aspects in the success of marketing processes and customer management. Training and motivating employees must be carefully planned and systematically assessed and monitored. Employees are not just a part but a component, of marketing.

Insurers need to incorporate a number of additional services into their insurance, which in being intrinsic to the insurance offered, are decisive in distinguishing between brands. This distinction requires an organisational culture that is customer-focused

The best insurance solutions that insurers can provide are those that from the start best integrate people, systems, technologies and processes, in response to the conscious and subconscious needs of customers.

Insurers need to recognise the importance of their employees in obtaining information on the quality of the experiences provided to the entities with which they relate. Employees are those who know and understand best what is good and bad in the customer interaction. Often customers identify employees as the only effective way to get their opinions, criticisms and suggestions across to the insurer.

The role of employees is also crucial in detecting anomalies in the services provided, before they become an issue, and also in taking advantage of opportunities for improvement.

Making the most of customer information is a unique motive for employees to get involved in their role as representatives of the insurer's values with those involved. Customer data must be consolidated with the information from employees so that insurers can evolve from the stage of understanding market dynamics to a higher level of knowledge of the underlying reasons for these dynamics.

Insurers need to avoid the most frequent obstacles in the way of employees transmitting customer information. These are:

- the disorganisation and disruption of data. The difficulties in consolidating data collected by different departments and stored in separate files seriously limits the collection and registration of information collected by employees;

- the reluctance of employees to share ideas, information and perceptions due to anxieties over a lack of security for the data collected and the identification of sources. Security measures must be installed to safeguard employees and customers from the negative impact caused by providing information. These measures must be made known inside and outside the insurance company.

- Little involvement of employees in the process of adding their knowledge to the insurance company's intelligence. A system of incentives is required to encourage employees to adopt a diligent attitude in the collection and recording of customer information. Employees should also be informed on how their contributions are processed.

The organisational culture

Employees should be willing and able to implement customer-first values in their daily activities. For these principles to become effective, the following conditions must be met:

- there must be a code of values and principles that show how important customers are to the insurer;

- employees equipped with the necessary awareness, preparation, training and education;

- measure the level to which these values are practised and act on results. A recommended good practice is to establish a direct relationship between results and the different awards attributed to employees.

The insurer must learn to listen to its customers, agents and its own employees.

There may be an internal perception that some customers do not deserve so much effort and commitment from employees as they undermine the insurer's profits. This reasoning is wrong, in that all employees must always act with the utmost dedication. The definition and shape of the value attributed to each customer segment is the responsibility of marketing or customer management.

The way in which employees act according to the standards demanded by the insurer, should not be an initiative or a project, but a natural practice, at all levels and in all operations. The insurer must be both ambitious and strict in this area, to ensure that all employees are aware that:

- all the tasks they carry out, regardless of their operations, have an impact (direct or indirect), on the experiences that are offered to customers;

- if customers are not satisfied with the experiences provided, they will not keep their insurance in force and they will they take out new insurance elsewhere, consequently undermining the insurer's profits.

A particularly effective exercise for employees in adopting a marketing culture is *deep diving*. This exercise makes all employees aware that the impact of their tasks goes far beyond the moment they conclude them. The exercise is in four phases:

> A. EACH EMPLOYEE IDENTIFIES ITS FIVE MOST IMPORTANT ACTIVITIES;
>
> B. FOR EACH ACTIVITY ARE LISTED THE MAIN IMPACTS ON THE VALUE THAT IS PROVIDED TO CUSTOMERS.
>
>> The inability to identify the impact of a task on the customer's experience can be interpreted in two ways:
>>
>> - employees fail to fully understand their task, meaning the insurer must teach them how to think creatively and innovatively;
>> - the task has no identifiable impact on the customer experience, which means either finding a way to make the task relevant or, if that fails, replace it by another task.
>
> C. IDENTIFY A DISRUPTIVE CHANGE THAT WILL MAKE EACH OF THE FIVE TASKS MORE IMPORTANT FOR THE CUSTOMER.
>
> D. FINALLY, REPLACE THE LEAST IMPORTANT TASK BY ONE MORE LIKELY TO BRING IMPROVEMENTS, OR REPLACE WITH A NEW TASK.

Figure 43: "Deep Diving" task process

The role of managers is crucial in the process of cultural change because of the guidance and example they provide. The entire insurance company should be structured in a way that makes these practices effective, at all levels and in particular:

- in designing careers and salary plans, rewarding good performance;

- in the way top managers perform their leadership, which cannot be as isolated autocratic decision-makers. The leader should adopt a profile that is visionary, strategic, educational and inspiring. It is also very important that department heads are encouraged to act in accordance with the principles of delegation of power, accountability and autonomy in the performance of operations.

The objective is to ensure that each employee is able consistently to provide quality services to customers, then reflected in positive experiences.

The selection of employees is often an underestimated factor in the insurer's ability to manage its customers. With effect from the selection phase, employees must have the behaviour and techniques compatible with the company's desired cultural standards. The absence of these conditions can lead to employees being unable to perform as required and this will have an immediate negative effect on customers and other external entities, as well as on colleagues, affecting the organisational climate as a whole. In the medium term, a deficient recruiting policy generates high rates of employee turnover, with serious repercussions for the insurer, given the importance of relationships with customers and agents to the success of the business.

The need to innovate is a decisive cultural aspect if insurers want to remain competitive. However, innovation must be developed from a customer and agent perspective, by opening the insurer to the market, rather than being based on its technical staff designing and launching new solutions. Innovation must cover all the insurer's operations because they all affect the time and manner in which interactions are established with customers and intermediaries.

Innovation should not be the result of an employee having a moment's inspiration and coming up with a good idea. Although not overlooking the importance of brilliant ideas, innovation must be a constant in the daily routine of the insurer and part of a process that assesses and tests proposals, in order to select those right for economic and social success, and then implement them.

It is the duty of all employees, at all levels, and of agents, to suggest how things could be done better or differently in order to generate better results.

Innovation is more productive the more the insurer is culturally geared to marketing. Human resources management policies must identify those employees concerned with innovation in the course of their work. Organisational structure often hinders innovation so that any obstacles in the way of new ideas and innovative proposals should be detected.

Lastly, information technology plays a decisive role in the process of innovation. Employees need access to accurate, complete customer information in order to identify the best opportunities to increase customer value.

<u>Intermediaries as an extension of the insurer</u>

In cases where there are intermediaries between the company and the end customer, the concern for human resource in the company should be extended to these intermediaries, ensuring that these business partners comply with the principles and values of the insurer.

The availability of indicators on how satisfied customers are with these intermediaries, and how individual results relate to best practices, is motivation for agents to adopt the insurer's principles. Rewarding these partners that achieve levels of excellence in customer satisfaction is something that should also be considered.

7F) Specific features of the insurance marketing-mix

Several features distinguish products from services. Insurance is a type of service with two particularly distinctive features:

- services are provided following the purchase, given that if there is no purchase, there will be no need for services. However, in over 80% of cases, the insurance is never used even after purchase, because no claims are ever made;

- the service is long term, given that its objective is to safeguard the personal and material well-being of clients.

In general terms, variables that characterise insurance services are as follows:

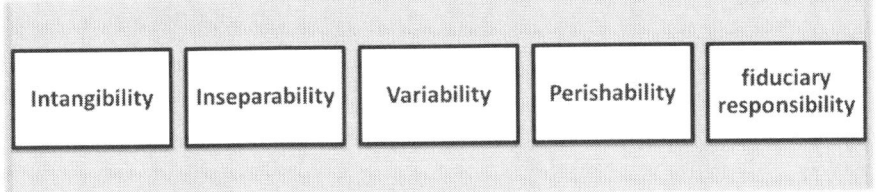

Figure 44: Specific features of insurance marketing-mix

7F1) Intangibility

The insurance may not be seen, felt, heard, smelt or touched; it can only be truly assessed after purchase and following the occurrence of a claim.

This means the insurance must materialise in the forms possible, through documentation and experience provided to customers.

The documentation given to customers (proposals, general conditions, collection-notification, receipts, among others), the attitude and behaviour of the insurer's employees and the attitude and competence of distribution channels are replacement indicators that are very much used by customers to assess the quality of services provided by the insurer.

7F2) Perishability

Insurance does not exist if it is not purchased by the customer, and it cannot be stored for future use.

This makes it difficult to adapt supply to demand, in that the capacity to produce insurance is not 'physically' exhausted (there is always a capacity to deliver more policies), however only by:

- restrictions resulting from reinsurance agreements;
- the culmination of risk, i.e. the maximum sum insured that an insurer can accept in respect of each coverage;

- the insurer's sum insured ratios.

From these values, assuming that there are no unusual circumstances in market operations, it is in the interest of the insurer to sell the maximum number of contracts, ensuring the balance of the portfolio and the spread of risks, in order to dilute the high fixed costs of insurance operations.

7F3) Inseparability

The production of insurance cannot be dissociated from its supplier. The configuration of the insurance sold (at all levels, such as cover, sums insured, deductibles or discounts), is the result of dealing between seller and buyer. The role of whoever sells the insurance in identifying, describing and quantifying the major risks that could affect the customer, as well as the best way to prevent them occurring and safeguarding the customer from them, is decisive to the quality of the sale, and consequently, to customer satisfaction with the insurance and with the insurer. For this reason, one aspect that must be managed carefully is the competence, training and motivation of the sales force.

The insurer can, in addition to the indicators for monitoring the business as a whole, assess sales quality by the volume of sales in non-compulsory insurance, voluntary cover and by the levels of customer satisfaction and loyalty.

One of the reasons why the Internet has gained in market share compared to other distribution channels, is the emergence of technological solutions that, without human intervention and using analytical models, present suggestions of safety solutions that are appropriate to the risk profile of each customer.

7F4) Heterogeneity

Given that the format of the insurance depends, as we have seen, on the result of the interaction between buyer and seller, and that all customers and vendors are different and behave differently according to circumstances, the solutions found for the protection of risks of each customer also vary.

Insurers endeavour to ensure that, regardless of the inherent variability of the sales process, the best safety solutions for each customer are found:

- "a priori", acting, for example, in the selection and hiring of employees and distributors, their training and the use of better processes and technologies;

- "a posteriori", using measures for analysis, such as:

    o sales quality, for example, looking at the turnover of non-compulsory insurance and coverage, average premiums and claims rates;

    o customer behaviour, for example, analysing how long they stay with the company and their share-of-wallet;

    o satisfaction surveys of customers and distribution channels;

    o mystery-shopping actions, in which an external entity plays the role of a customer and assesses the quality of customer service provided;

    o audits of processes, particularly those most relevant to the quality of services provided to customers and agents and which are critical for the management of the insurer.

In this way, Insurers are able to minimise the risk of their employees adopting the wrong attitude in dealing with customers, distribution channels and other members of the local community.

7F5) Fiduciary responsibility

Fiduciary responsibility is a specific feature of financial products, and is due to the activity being based on customer risk management and fund management, in the long-term.

The reliability and stability of the insurer, transmitted by its employees and managers, as well as by its representatives and communications, are essential for customers to purchase an insurer's solutions that will consequently lead to its success.

7G) The brand

The brand is an intangible asset, and extremely important and valuable to insurers. It consists of a perception, formed in the minds of those to whom the insurer relates, of brand value. All symbols, signs, communications and references concerning the insurer, its insurance, employees, shareholders and partners, contribute to shaping this perception. How customers interpret the references to the brand may be different, depending on their characteristics and their circumstances. It is crucial for the brand to be managed in the same strict and scientific way as other important and valuable assets.

The brand creates a favourable predisposition in the relationship with customers, partners and employees, and without doubt generates the best results when it is studied, monitored and managed. Insurers need to create the right conditions, and have the means, knowledge, and skills to manage their brand, so as to develop their own competitive advantage. People relate to brands for what they represent, despite their being intangible, rather than to the insurance itself.

Insurers do not always give adequate priority to managing their brand or do not have the know-how to manage it, which is a mistake, in that a strong brand brings several benefits to insurers, such as:

- more loyalty from customers, employees and agents;

- ability to apply higher average premiums, generating higher profit margins;

- ability to create higher barriers to the entry of competitors;

- easier diversification of business and attraction of new customer segments.

The fiduciary nature of insurance and the fact that it is a business where the significant perception of risk associated with purchase highlights the need for brand management. The brand image is, as previously indicated, one of the main replacement indicators used by customers in making their purchase decisions.

Customer management should not be confused with brand management. Although the themes are related, their goals are different. Companies that are geared to brand management are focused on the stakeholders' view of the insurer and its products. In guiding customer management the brand is a powerful tool in retaining the most valuable customers, in increasing the value of the relationship and in attracting new high potential customers.

In short, investment in the brand should not be a goal in itself, but a means to creating and strengthening relationships with those to whom the insurer relates.

7G1) The importance of brands in the insurance sector

A brand is a perception generated in a person's mind of the extent to which an entity (individual or company) delivers the promised benefits. This mental image, completely intangible, is more easily remembered if embodied in sensorial elements, which may be visual (logos or colours), auditory (such as jingles) or olfactory stimuli (such as, for example, the aromas associated with nature or close relationships). However, these elements are important only to the extent they amplify the presence of the brand, and should not be confused with the central elements of brand management. We often make the mistake of confusing the process of monitoring how logos, colours, signatures or jingles are used, with the actual management of the insurance brand.

Customers buy insurance from a company because they believe they are going to benefit, which in value terms makes it better than any other known alternative.

The fundamental concern of the brand is to deliver its implicit and explicit promises. It is a mistake to think that major brand issues are resolved through communication, changing logos, refreshing websites or reformulating the advertising. The factors that are normally associated with brand management such as, names, logos, advertising or public relations, are the ways in which the promise made by the brand is expressed and not the core activity of fulfilling the explicit and implicit promise that it makes. The best managed brands are those that fulfil their promises, and that achieve them through positive experiences.

Insurance is one of the businesses where brand management is more important because its object is the management of expectations in the sense that the promises sold will be fulfilled.

The human mind processes information in an extremely efficient way, through the recognition and interpretation of patterns. The brand acts as a clue, and when consistent, generates an automatic association with the values associated with it. The brand provides symbolic clues that raise the customer's expectation of certain types of benefit. The association of clues, expectations and experiences, is the determining factor in brand management, because customers adopt consistent brands and ignore or dismiss inconsistent brands.

The importance of brand identity is, therefore, crucial as clue that triggers the process of mental associations with the expected benefits and consequently its value to the customer. Either way, the clue is just the triggering factor for identification and not the substance of the brand.

It is important to distinguish the brand promise from its positioning. The promise refers to the objective of the brand or its reason to exist, while its positioning distinguishes it from competitors and makes it relevant. Positioning refers to the space within the competitive domain that the brand wants to occupy. The promise takes a further step in relation to positioning in being a commitment to the customer to provide value in a certain way. The promise is the bridge that links expectations with experiences, distinguishing what it will provide from what it will not provide. Positioning is by nature much more changeable than promise, in that it is much more easily copied, and so must be regularly reinvented.

It is better to resist the temptation to try to satisfy the expectations of all customers, because, inevitably, expectations will be frustrated, reducing the brand's credibility and consequently destroying its value.

Many brands are tempted to react to market trends or customer preferences through constant repositioning. This approach often reduces the value of the brand, creating confusion among customers and hindering the development of brand objectives.

The idea that customers usually remember the visual aspects of brands is wrong and can lead to re-branding projects based on creating attractive logos and colour patterns that are in fashion. The fact is that if the experience does not meet brand promises, the visual elements will not place the brand in the customer's evoked set, and so will become irrelevant.

7G2) Types of insurance brand

A universally applicable model of brand categorisation[14], of particular interest in understanding insurance brands, sorts them into:

---

[14] Adapted from Laurence Vincent, 2012

- Cultural - brands that are associated first of all with the patterns of a particular culture. This pattern has to be shared with all brand representatives (in particular employees, shareholders and distributors) and affects all organisational operations. The "Liberty Mutual Group" brand, for example, is strongly linked to North American cultural patterns.

- Addressed - in that the brand represents the fundamental value that the organisation wants to achieve, for example, German efficiency represented by Allianz or the Swiss precision of Zurich.

- Functional - brands focused on aspects of their commercial proposals. The Progressive Group, for instance, claims to provide "Immediate claims response when you need it most".

- Ingredients - when the brand is used for valuing another commercial proposal.

- Insurers can, for example, turn to customer service companies, car rental services, and hospitals within their network, or even to reinsurers, as its ingredients. On the other hand, if these entities adopt a clear positioning in a certain field, such as stability, reliability or meeting commitments, they can use the insurer brand to add credibility to their own initiatives.

What is important is that brands are not necessarily exclusive to one category, and may fall into two or more classes. On the other hand, being classified in one category does not preclude being included in another.

7G3) The benefits of brands

The customer's mind assesses the benefits offered by brands several times a day, although this is mainly a subconscious process. The brands influence this process decisively, although they are only effective when they provide a relevant benefit to the customer.

Insurers need to be committed to meeting their promises, using the most realistic, innovative way possible, basing their benefits on one of the following core areas[15]:

Accessibility

The benefit consists of turning the insurance offer into something more approachable, by:

- reducing the price;

- being placed in multiple sale locations, such as with many agents or bank branches, post offices, stores and outlets for other businesses, and the internet.

In insurance, accessibility is a type of recurring benefit valued by customers, among other reasons because of ease of access to the insurer in case of a claim.

Functionality

Brands focus their promises on allocating more and better functional characteristics. While the accessible brands may relinquish some features to maximise ease of purchase for customers, the functional brands address customers that prefer brands with a better performance in the areas they value most. The brand is not characterised by having more features but by providing exceptional performance in the features offered.

Personality

All brands have their personality. This dimension of the brand, much more profound than its functional characteristics, is revealed when customers perceive it according to psychographic traits (such as, being reliable, ambitious, stable or transparent). The critical success factor is to ensure that

---

[15] Adapted from Laurence Vincent, 2012

all employees identify and embody this personality at all times. The association of the brand with public figures that embody the traits of personality with which the brand identifies, is one of the more effective communication tactics.

<u>Life Style</u>

The brand embodies or contributes to the customer attaining certain social aspirations. The purchasing process, or use of the brand, generates a benefit that consists of a feeling of belonging to a particular social or cultural segment. It is an irrational aspiration, in the sense that the benefits are not clearly measurable. In this case, customers do not buy insurance policies, but rather an entry pass to a particular group. When all is said and done, customers expect that the life style to which they aspire will become part of their reality.

This type of benefit provided by the insurance is less frequent, although it is probably the area in which insurance marketing has most development potential.

Brands must understand in which of these four areas they are positioned. These areas evolve in terms of their growing irrationality and the importance of emotional involvement, and brands position themselves according to the level to which they wish to rise. For this reason the insurer must assess its competitors and, above all, its employees (what motivates them and where their best skills lie) and customers.

The insurer must be able to provide the benefits promised on a consistent basis in all interactions with any entity. The overwhelming majority of insurers face the challenge of evolving from providing functional benefits (where markets tend to be less profitable) to the more irrational areas.

<u>7G4) Management of insurer brands</u>

Managing an insurers brand involves five points of action, as shown in figure 45:

- architecture of relations among brands;

- identifying platform;

- valuation of brand portfolio;

- control of reputation;

- contingency plan.

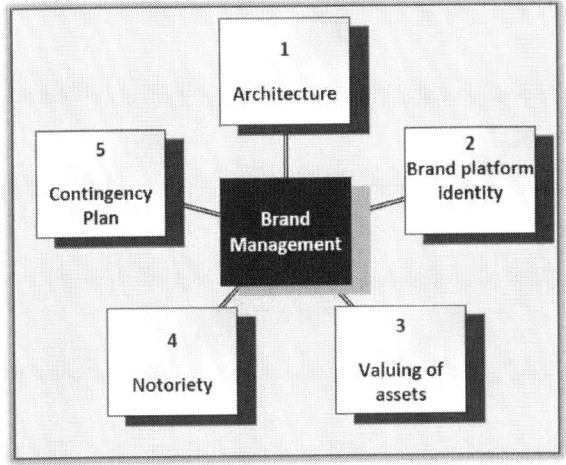

Figure 45: Central Aspects of insurance brand management

The architecture of inter-brand relations

Consistency is vital in the architecture of insurer brands, so that overall brand value is maximised and its identity clearly perceived by the local community.

The architecture of brands consists of defining the organisational structure that establishes how brands in a portfolio relate and, at the same time, how they differ. Brands can be created, destroyed and repositioned, but all these moves must be framed within a system that ensures an increase in portfolio value.

The three fundamental brand architecture models are as follows[16]:

- Independent brands. In this case the brand names do not relate neither to one another nor to the insurer brand. The main advantages of this option are:

    - providing considerable positioning freedom to each brand;
    - reducing conflicts between distribution channels;
    - preventing the danger of contamination between brands.

- Endorsed brands. In this situation, the names of brands are independent from one another but contain some element that relates them. This option, although a possible happy medium between independent brands and endorsed brands, requires less investment in reputation but allows less freedom for positioning than independent brands.

- Umbrella brands. This model is the most common in the insurance sector and includes the name of the insurer under the insurance brand. The main advantage of this model is that it generates large synergies between brands, requiring less investment in its communication and positioning.

---

[16] Aaker, Joachimsthaler

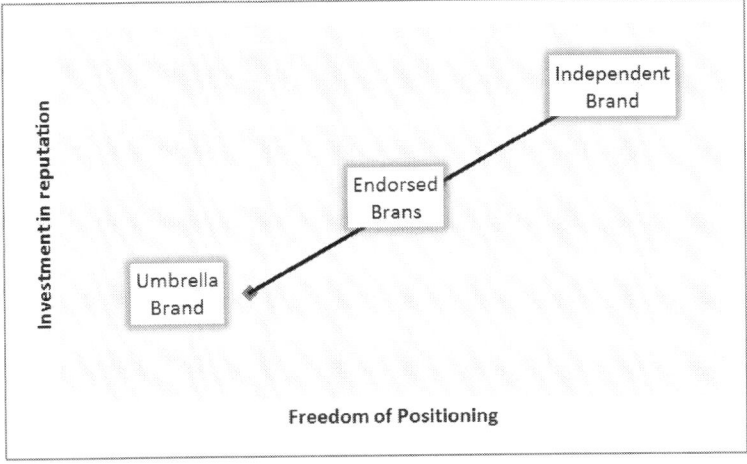

Figure 46: Models of brand architecture

The identity platform of brands

Brand identity embodies the consistency of its promises, reflected in the experiences it provides. Identity is instrumental in brand management and should only be changed when it no longer reflects the brand promise.

The identity platform determines the purpose of the brand by defining the reason for its existence. In the long term, it represents a vital protection and an instrument of continuity. Paradoxically, being aware of brand identity confers greater freedom of expression on brand management, because it emphasises its substantial aspects and formal characteristics, distinguishing what can be changed from what should not be changed.

Logos, colours and signature are elements that, together with the name, give the brand its identity.

The brand name is an important component of its identity, but no more than that. Reality has demonstrated that almost all names are good, providing they do not contain a negative connotation or are difficult to pronounce.

In the process of verifying a name, it must be tested carefully because no matter what name is suggested there are always good reasons for rejecting it. Sometimes names mean nothing but the sound of the name is pleasing to customers, and could be a good choice.

The brand logo is also sometimes wrongly confused with the essence of brand management. It is an important symbol, with a content that should be changing to accompany the associations it evokes, but it is no more than a way of representing the brand.

The key to brand identity symbols is that they should only be used when there is a guarantee that the brand experience is consistent with its promise. The insurer's logo should not be entrusted to any of the insurer's agents and representatives until mechanisms are put in place to monitor the quality of experience offered (as described in the chapter on experience management).

<u>Optimizing the brand portfolio</u>

Insurer brands may evolve in several ways. In each case, opportunities for development should be assessed, taking their main opportunities, threats and vulnerabilities into consideration.

Possible moves to develop the brand further[17]:

- by extension, in launching new brands from existing ones. The main advantage is to gain access to new areas with less investment in communication. The disadvantages are limiting any gain from the potential scale of the new brand and risking the mother brand becoming vulnerable.

- repositioning the brand involves a high risk to the insurer. To succeed, customers must forget the initial positioning of the brand to later

---

[17] Hill, Lederer.

grasp a different position. This option does usually apply to a single brand, but to the insurer's portfolio.

- The *Insights* campaign associated with the *Zurich Help-Point* concept, launched in 2008 and reinforced in 2010, in over 40 countries, marked a new approach for Zurich to relate to its customers.

- suppressing a brand. This option may be crucial for the long-term success of the brand portfolio. The following consequences of this option should be considered:

    o abandoning the strategic space that becomes available to competitors;

    o the loss of investment in creating and developing the brand.

- co-branding is an association with the brand of an entity outside the insurer's portfolio.

- up-scaling the brand by filling a new strategic space on the upper or lower fringes of the insurer's positioning.

Reputation management

Brand value depends to a large extent on the brand's reputation. All investments in creating the brand and adding value to it are lost if customers and other entities do not recognise the brand. A brand with no reputation is of no value and is an irrelevant appendix to the insurer.

The three main types of reputation are distinguished by how customers relate to the insurer when they are questioned about insurance or how risks can be prevented. The main assumptions are:

- top of mind, which takes place when the brand is the customer's first reference;

- spontaneous reputation, when the brand is one of the references indicated by customers;

- assisted reputation, when the brand is recognised by the customer after a reference has been made to it.

The relative importance of the three types of reputation will vary depending on the stage of the customer decision process and the customer's degree of involvement with the insurance. Each type of reputation serves to achieve different goals and requires separate investment in communications. Placing an insurer at top of the mind requires considerably more investment than if the goal is to add a higher degree of assisted reputation.

Top of mind is very important in the sale of insurance via the Internet and in cases where the customer is scarcely involved in the purchase. In this case, the customer accesses the first site that comes to mind. This means the insurer must know how to position itself as the customer's first reference because this is a critical success factor.

Spontaneous reputation is very important, for example, in purchases through comparison sites (*aggregators*). These Internet sites show the customer the cheaper insurance available for a given combination of cover. Although price is usually the decisive factor in purchasing via this channel, customers must be familiar with the brand. If they are not, they may choose another slightly less expensive brand that they recognise.

Assisted reputation is very important when the purchase is made through agents. In this situation, it is essential that when the agent introduces a certain insurance to the customer, that the brand is not totally unknown.

<u>The contingency plan</u>

Brand management should have a contingency plan to protect its main risks. Risks may involve rumours and negative comments made about the brand in the digital social media and these can be highly destructive to the brand and they spread quickly.

8) Marketing Information Systems

Good customer information is essential for the efficiency of all insurance operations, and not just marketing, because all departments make decisions that affect, and are influenced by, the value and characteristics of customers.

There cannot be strong, mutually beneficial relationships between two entities that do not know one another. Poor quality data means insurers are unable to describe the sensations, perceptions and customer profiles of its customers.

To be competitive insurers must adopt the necessary measures to improve the quality, quantity and reliability of the information on all entities, particularly:

- identifying cross-selling and retention opportunities, with a consequent increase in customer value;

- providing information, at all points of contact with the customers to help establish dialogue that is of value to the insurer, the customer and the agent;

- guaranteeing that all employees have the same consistent and up-dated information;

- improving corporate governance models to keep the insurer in compliance with regulatory requirements.

The inability to understand customers, and consequently to manage them, is the result of cultural and organisational factors, such as:

- the absence of a clear perception of the importance of customer data;

- a lack of skills and experience in managing information on all entities;

- the absence of investment in the collection, processing and storage of customer data.

Contrary to what happens in other sectors, such as banking, in which most contracts are officially completed in the company providing the service, most insurance contracts are not completed at the premises of insurers, limiting control over how the transaction support documents are filled in.

Agents should be made aware of the importance of providing reliable, detailed customer data to the insurer. The focus of the agent's business in providing personal support to customers and in achieving short term business goals, detracts from other aspects.

In these circumstances customers are not treated according to their value, business opportunities are lost, and the relationship with the best customers jeopardised and resources wasted, all of which leads to a loss in profits.

Insurers need to know about all interactions involving their customers, such as requests for information, complaints, purchased insurance, claims or payments, to add this to other demographic and behavioural data they already have.

Success in business depends increasingly on scientific activities that tend to be more successful the better the techniques and tools available are used. These techniques apply, regardless of the insurance sector or the distribution or communication channel.

Many companies are preparing to compete in this environment by acquiring new systems dedicated to customer management, but they do not have enough customer data, which is the raw material for this system to operate.

In the same way that the secret to a good meal is the quality of its ingredients, it is the same for the strategic management of customers, no matter how sophisticated the support systems are, appropriate, sufficient data is necessary for the insurer to produce practical results.

Besides ensuring the quality of the information gathered in the initial customer contact, processes must be implemented to up-date this information, given the increasing frequency with which this information will change throughout the customer's life span.

Having good customer data is a key goal for all insurers, despite being a task that is never complete given that:

- customer rotation is high, up to 30% a year in some markets and for some types of insurance;

- customer data changes:

    o in the case of individuals, their address, marital status, professional situation, or even their name;

    o in the case of companies, the number of employees, the geographical locations of their business operations.

In order to interact with the right customers, providing the correct proposals, at the right time, information must be up-to-date, complete and reliable. Given that customer information is constantly changing, it has to be carefully managed.

Surprisingly, few insurers have anyone, or anything, responsible for managing customer information, but such management is essential for the highly reliable data required for the insurer's intensive, mass use.

The absence of responsibility for customer information management is reflected throughout the insurance company: in everyday interactions with its own customers and agents, in strategic planning and in dealings with shareholders and supervisors.

Responsibility for this information must be incorporated into customer management. The insurer's main use of customer information is in its dealings with the local community, so that responsibility for its management must lie with whichever department is responsible for relations management. Technological infrastructures are also critical for storing and processing data, another area that should come under the responsibility of information technology systems.

8A) Fundamental customer data

Insurers already deal with large quantities of data from different sources, such as:

- internal to the insurer, in the different departments within its structure;
- official agencies;
- specialised companies;
- social media[18].

However, much data important to customer management is not obtained because its value is not recognised and it does not even get loaded into the insurer's data processing systems.

Besides demographic, geographic, socio-economic, cultural[19] and transactional information (resulting from customer interactions with the insurer) that exist in most information systems, the following types of data should be given considerable attention:

- electronic means of contact, such as e-mail addresses and personal web pages, because they are vehicles of communication that are increasingly indispensable in customer interactions;

---

[18] As described in the chapter "Auto-segmentation".
[19] Detailed in the "Segmentation" chapter.

- the hobbies of individual customers and decision-makers in companies, which besides being important to the life of these people, are a unique way of determining character, providing valuable pointers to business and communication opportunities;

- profession, which although provided in social and cultural data, is information often ignored, although it also helps identify the customers professional category and business sector;

- immediate family members, identifying names, gender and ages, given the crucial role they play in the customer decisions of the family group;

- relationships (professional, family or other) between individuals. This information is usually ignored, despite being crucial for a correct customer description. It may be that the individual analysis of a customer value is negative, overlooking that this customer could be a close family member of another very valuable customer, or one with a very important position in a company that is highly important to the insurer. It may also be that a customer is wrongly identified as a potential purchaser for an insurance that he already has, because this product meets the group's requirements (as financial, home or motor insurance), and not only individual.

A correct customer analysis must also incorporate data that assesses customer perception, motivation and attitude towards the insurer, such as complaints or satisfaction level.

All customer information will be greatly enhanced if consolidated with environmental elements that relate to customer behaviour in certain circumstances.

Lastly, customer information management must comply with the legal obligation to register with data protection and privacy agencies.

8B) Customer data management

Measures adopted to ensure the quality and quantity of customer data include:

- monitoring and processing existing data;
- obtaining missing information.

These processes can be carried out at different intervals, focusing on different types of data, and covering the whole or only a part of the insurer's customers. Often there is no justification for the widespread application of all measures, to all customers, and the characteristics of customers that justify implementing each measure must be defined.

Some customer information management measures must be constantly implemented, while others need only be implemented at certain times. Here are some examples of actions that fall under these categories.

8B1) Permanent measures to ensure the quality of data

Measures that must be constantly implemented are the following:

- carrying out data control tests by sampling, to determine the vulnerabilities that exist in the different phases of the process of obtaining and recording information;

- verification and validation of fields, at the time they are recorded, such as dates, warnings of exceptional cases (customers over the age of 100 or under the age of 18) or gender not being consistent with first name;

- control of redundancies at time of registration, by identifying new entities where there is a high likelihood that they are repetitions of others that already exist;

- decentralisation of the capacity to complete, update and correct customer data, particularly at points of sale and at insurance offices;

- availability of forms for data up-date, in all places of contact with customers, granting awards or incentives for filling them in.

8B2) Frequent measures to ensure the quality of data

With a regularity that may vary from monthly to six-monthly, the following procedures should be implemented:

- assess whether there are gaps between the information necessary for customer management and data collected, identifying ways to overcome this situation;

- ask customers directly by phone, *e-mail* or personally, to fill in the empty fields and correct any incorrect data, possibly in exchange for incentives;

- audit errors entered in introducing data at each phase of the process and for each participant, and implement preventative measures to avoid their occurring;

- complement the insurer's promotional measures and public relations with initiatives for obtaining customer data;

- take advantage of information available in documents or e-mails received from customers to complete or check existing data.

8B3) Occasional measures to ensure the quality of data

The following procedures should be implemented half-yearly or annually:

- harmonise repeated records for the same entity;

- ensure that all means of collecting customer data, from insurance proposals to records on Internet sites, request the same fields in accordance with the same rules;

- monitor data input circuits, identifying processes that generate systematic errors and how to overcome them;

- convert information systematically loaded into free text fields into closed response fields.

8C) Technological infrastructure

Technological infrastructure is essential for the staff of the insurance company, duly prepared and trained for the task, to process customer data into information the insurer can use and add to.

Customer data processing systems are contained in data-marts where information is concentrated and consolidated, regardless of its origins, for immediate access and use in complex analyses. If there is no such infrastructure the insurer is restricted in managing its customers:

- data selection becomes fallible, complex and time consuming;

- it becomes impossible to obtain a true and comprehensive picture of each customer;

- it ignores the results of prior measures as it is unable to incorporate knowledge from previous experiences, halting further development of the customer's information system.

The provision of a unified, integrated vision of the customer is therefore the fundamental challenge of the infrastructure technology that supports customer management.

In certain circumstances, the creation of these information files and how to access them (the *data-mart* and *date-warehouse*), can involve more time and resources than the insurer has available. In these cases it is advisable to create simpler data bases associated with the most rudimentary processes for customer information unification and processing, with data models mapped directly to the insurer's central systems, creating an initial solution for the launch of the first initiatives. Later, this solution will evolve, adding transactional data and other customer information obtained through the different communication and distribution channels.

Once completed, this step will provide a harmonised, integrated vision of the customer throughout the entire insurance company. With this infrastructure, the insurer will be able to approach its customers in a distinctive way, with significant benefits for all parties concerned:

- identifying customer preferences and acting on this knowledge;

- adding visibility to issues that affect the relationship with key customers, attacking the sources of dissatisfaction before they cause abandonment;

- increasing the speed and flexibility of the insurer's response to environmental changes, and the challenges of its competitors in particular;

- improving the agent's ability to serve its customers, with the best advice and suggestions to protect them from their major risks.

9) The social media

The social media publish content via digital platforms available on the Internet.

The disruptive factor to the social media is that any user can create, distribute and obtain information and establish relationships, with complete transparency, without barriers, without any censorship and without content limitation, apart from the constraints of:

- the capacity of the equipment and computer applications being used;
- applicable legislation;
- restrictions dictated by its own ethical principles.

Insurers use the social media, although not developing any particular processes for this. Whenever someone refers to the insurer critically, makes a comment or asks a question, than the insurer is present in the social media.

Once this phase has been overcome, several insurers have remained at the following level: they have decided to be present on social media, but without interacting with the surrounding media community. This option is not advisable because it is perceived by customers as the insurer's ignorance of social networks and a wish to avoid confrontation with unfavourable opinions regarding its insurance business.

The correct stand is not to inhibit or limit users from expressing themselves, but to grant freedom of expression, the insurer monitoring, listening and assessing comments made, so that, whenever necessary, misunderstandings can be cleared up.

Despite the volatility of the whole social media universe, with new platforms and communities appearing and disappearing rapidly and frequently, it is clear that the social media is changing the way in which insurance companies interact and do business.

This is a topic that needs to be sustained in a strategy, although it may be shaped contrary to traditional processes, in that:

- it is the customer that often triggers the contact process by referring, questioning, commenting or challenging the insurer;
- it is the customer that is self-segmenting in opting to join certain virtual communities and the way they are accessed.

All the insurer's employees should know the insurer is present in the social media because any of them could be targeted for questions or comments. Their reactions in responding should always be compatible with the objectives and the positioning of the insurer because as targets they are not individuals as private individuals, but as employees of the insurer.

9A) Social media: an inevitable reality

The social media has an increasingly important role to play in developing the insurer's brand, its prestige, reputation and its ability to do business. The challenge facing insurers is no longer when they will join the social media, but how they will perform.

The social media opens significant opportunities for insurance business by congregating on a common platform all entities to which the insurer relates, facilitating the launch of new solutions, cross-selling of its insurance, the retention of its customers and even the recovery of lost customers.

A firm approach to the social media, providing users with a good experience, creates a favourable attitude that can convert users into promoters of the insurer's strong points. However, the reverse is also true. If, for example, the insurer's employees act inappropriately or if they use inadequate processes, users will have bad experiences that may be transmitted and spread among their contacts.

From the onset insurers need to develop the skills required to maintain a presence in the social media, particularly the human and technological resources that help establish and maintain relationships in these new areas.

However, the social media is not just another means of contact with customers, working with rules similar to other media. The social media is a different way of being in the market and doing business, affecting all insurer processes in the following ways:

- speed of decision-making and implementation of solutions. Everything happens in real time, with a propagation speed that does not allow for switching off the insurer's activity at 5pm on a Friday to return at 9am the following Monday;

- transparency. The impact of an employee's failure in dealing with a customer, a situation that in another context could lead to a simple complaint, can now take on huge proportions. The clarity of procedures is crucial in preventing the occurrence of any possible misunderstanding, and should this occur it must be justified, in order to convince the customer affected, and the remaining community, that the insurer was involved in finding the best possible solution to the situation;

- the technological ability to collect, process and transform the large quantities of data generated in monitoring the presence of the insurer and its stakeholders in the social media, into usable information;

- improving the understanding of its customers, segmenting them according to traditional criteria with its self-segmenting criteria technique, dictated by its online profile.

In terms of concept, there are two organisational models that insurance companies can use to deal with social media challenges:

- centralised, with responses coordinated by a specific component, which is normally established in the marketing department. This centre of competencies is composed of a multidisciplinary, multifunctional team, acting as organiser and controller of all interactions that are established between the insurer and the surrounding community.

    This body is responsible for ensuring consistency in all processes and interactions, defining service levels for the insurer's operations in the social media and guaranteeing that they comply;

- distributed across several organisational departments. This model is less common and is generally experimental, and from here it evolves into a centralised model. This option contains various risks due to the absence of a single coordinator to regulate and control the whole system.

The responsibility for managing social media programmes has been assigned mainly to marketing, the department most skilled to interact with the different target groups and with responsibility for boosting the presence of the insurer in the social media. However, this is not a challenge unique to marketing, but to the insurer as a whole, involving all its operations, and cooperation among all departments is essential. The insurer has to ensure that the programme is conducted carefully and with know-how, in all aspects, so that any issue that arises can be dealt with by the most competent employees.

The leadership and coordination of the people involved in the insurer's social media should be the responsibility of marketing, which publicises and promotes this programme to other departments highlighting:

- how it operates;

- its importance and the increased responsibilities that it entails for both individuals and teams, throughout the company;

- its main opportunities and threats.

9B) Principal forms of social media

The digital social media comes in different forms, reaching different target groups and achieving different business goals for insurers. The main forms of social media are the following:

- blogs;
- micro-blogs;
- social networks;
- media sharing sites;
- forums.

9B1) Blogs

A blog is a contents management system for publishing small articles, known as *posts*.

This means is not suitable for formal communications from insurers or for the commercial promotion of their insurance. Insurers should use blogs to disseminate and comment on events occurring in the business, the relevant activities in which the company is involved or the news that affects the lives of people and the competitiveness of companies.

It is not advisable to create a blog if the insurer is unable to:

- refresh high frequency contents;
- have the knowledge, skills and experience required to develop content that is relevant and interesting for users and be able to establish dialogues with experts:

- have the capacity to develop an innovative theme, interesting for the target audience, related to the insurance business, and that is not sufficiently exploited by other blogs.

9B2) Micro-blogs

Micro-blogs are a variation of blogs, particularity limited in size, which can be measured by the number of characters in the *posts*.

The most successful micro-blogging channel is Twitter. This medium has huge potential for use in the insurance sector in:

- providing relevant information on the safety or mitigation of risks to individuals and businesses;
- publishing news headlines, with links to other resources where the contents are developed;
- disseminating initiatives, campaigns and promotions.

Insurers must have as many activities and publish as many tweets as possible, providing they are all relevant, to demonstrate their involvement with the community of followers.

The insurer's success on Twitter can be assessed by the number of followers it has. In addition, and perhaps most important, is the measure of the extent to which these followers are involved, so that the number and type of references that are made and the amount of re-tweets (which means the tweets forwarded), are the most important assessment measures of the insurer's presence on Twitter.

9B3) Social networks

Social networks are the digital media used to develop networking for their users, both personal and professional. These resources are also available for companies, and insurers can use them to communicate with the communities of which they are part, bearing in mind that each medium has its own working rules, and these must be complied with for the potential and opportunities of these networks to be used to the full.

Facebook is the most popular and widespread network of social contacts. On Facebook insurers can create their own pages and publish content with a minimum of institutional information, but providing informative and instructive material.

In this environment, the challenge for insurers is to encourage the public to become fans and to visit its website regularly, which given the nature of relationships involved in the insurance business, is a task both difficult and challenging.

LinkedIn is a social network of professional contacts with larger numbers of users throughout Europe and America. Its scope is vast and, unlike other networks of professional contacts, it is not restricted to any professional category or business sector.

The basic measure of assessing success from a presence on social networks is the number of users who join the group or become fans of the insurer. The likes, comments, shares, searches and references made to a page or publication should all be monitored.

9B4) Media sharing sites

This type of social media includes websites where users disclose their multimedia content.

YouTube

YouTube is distinct in this category as the site with the greatest number of users and videos, and is one of the most visited sites on the Internet.

These sites are very important for insurance companies because they provide content that is attractive and interesting, and ensure a high level of user interaction with their message. Users need to be involved with the insurer or with the contents of the message to access a specific video, selecting from all available alternatives. However, as with most other social media, there is very little tolerance for content that is strictly commercial.

One of the most powerful techniques to ensure a presence on YouTube is by making the insurer's videos available for use by anonymous users, allowing them, under certain conditions, to disclose the contents to their contacts on this or other media.

In insurance marketing courses, for example, insurer videos available on YouTube are often used to illustrate course content. This practice benefits students, by consolidating their theoretical knowledge with real cases, and insurers, because their messages are displayed and analysed by an audience of potential insurance marketing specialists.

Flickr
Flickr is probably the best known website for sharing images. It is a very good media for insurers to publish content associated with its own insurance business, such as risk behaviour that should be avoided and their impact on people and companies, as long as this content is not essentially commercial.

Slideshare
Slideshare is a website for sharing presentations, which as in other media for document sharing requires the content to be both attractive and interesting. However, users only select and watch the presentations that attract them so that content will only be fully viewed if it attracts users to the presentation, and subsequently to the insurer.

The main measure of success of the insurer's presence on content-sharing sites is the number of hits it gets, which is the number of times the site is accessed and browsed. Counting users that have commented or shared content on their sites or pages is another effective measure of the insurer's presence on this communication media.

9B5) Forums

Forums are the oldest digital social environment. They consist of sites for discussion and for sharing opinions and knowledge, usually specialising in a particular theme, or with members who share similar features, affinities or common interests.

Insurers must identify the forums that relate best to their business and that fall within the scope of their position, so that their participation is regular, informed and competent, making their knowledge and experience available to the community, without making their commercial objectives known.

The decision to start a new discussion forum should be considered very carefully. Besides requiring a significant investment in time, resources and technologies, it requires the ability to attract a high number of participants for future connections and relationships.

There is usually more benefit in investing in the presence of the insurer in the leading forums that have already achieved significant success with their target users, rather than creating a new forum.

The most basic measure of the insurer's presence in forums is the number of publications the insurer has edited, and the number of comments targeting them.

9C) Insurance in social media

A presence in the social media requires a significant investment in time, resources and people. It is essential to have a detailed plan that guides, structures and schedules the necessary changes for the insurer to implement and monitor this presence. Implementation involves five phases:

1) an understanding of the written and unwritten rules of operation;

2) being aware of audience profiles and the definition of those in which the insurer wants to have an active presence;

3) setting the objectives for the insurer's presence;

4) defining the insurer's stand;

5) determining the metrics for monitoring the insurer's presence in the social media.

The first step to actively participating in the social media consists of knowing the rules, particularly the unwritten rules, for each medium. The comments, published references and profile of participating members must be understood, particularly of the most active and influential. Insurers need to be aware of the references made to their brand, their main competitors and the insurance business.

References and reviews involving the insurer must be monitored carefully, given the impact this has on the brand.

Any talk in the social media related to the insurer and the insurance business must be identified and understood, and, in broader terms, anything related to the financial sector and risk management. The insurer needs to know the key influencers in any such talk as well as the specific issues being addressed.

Ratings, *rankings and* reviews are important to insurer success in these areas. Users attach much importance to these indicators in their assessment of insurers and insurance.

The second step consists of knowing the profile of the audience on each medium. To have a complete picture of the people that access each site, the profiles of known entities should be cross checked with the insurer's own internal information on such users, in order to classify their comments, behaviour patterns and attitudes.

After determining the main sites the insurer should follow, the necessary conditions for monitoring the media must be put in place, internally or with external partners.

In third place, the insurer must establish the goals it wants to achieve by its presence in the social media environment, which result from its positioning.

At the initial stage, the insurer should avoid areas where it is in some way vulnerable in its practices or communication policies.

The goals are gradually revised as the insurer extends the scope of its presence in the social media and acquires more knowledge and experience of each medium.

In fourth place, the insurer must define the stand it wants to adopt in the social media. In general there are two types of stand:

- non-commercial or passive, adopted by developing and publishing content in different social media to strengthen and boost the reputation of brand value, but without specific sales goals;

- commercial or active that aims, in addition to the passive approach, to develop measures under a commercial development plan, designed with specific goals and time-lines.

    Insurer campaigns can be based on the social media or may include the social media with the traditional media in a multi-channel platform.

    There are special events, such as a major claim, or commemorative dates such as Christmas or Mother's Day, which can also be leveraged to launch these initiatives.

Regardless of the stand adopted by the insurer, the various social media are not independent of one another. Most users are on more than one medium, which means the insurer should adopt an integrated, consolidated approach, consistent with an entire universe of possibilities.

One of the most important insurer decisions in handling the social media is whether or not to react to comments it receives, and if it does, how to go about this. This is very important in the insurance business because it often gives rise to conflict between those involved for several reasons, but above all because of the complexity of the insurance itself, lack of trust resulting from fraud warnings, or the lack of technical expertise of some employees and agents.

There are three guiding principles to deciding on when and how the insurer should react to references made:

- most comments and opinions expressed about the insurer reflect the opinion of people who may be poorly informed on matters they do not understand. It is clear that such comments may also be ill-intentioned, but the insurer must begin with the assumption that this is not the case and always respond constructively;

- the risk of an inappropriate reaction could significantly increase the negative effect of an irrelevant issue;

- the need to avoid the insurer adopting a superior role, which, in itself alone, would not be well received by users.

In the case of a negative reference resulting from a minor problem that customer services can resolve, the response should come from this service. If the reference is more serious, with significant potential damage to the brand, a balanced approach should be adopted, neither too defensive nor too aggressive, through the medium that carried the initial comment.

Negative reviews that degrade the insurer's image should be dealt with in such a way as to change dissatisfaction into satisfaction, with the insurer encouraging a further comment, but this time positive. This is a way of avoiding an issue, that portrays the insurer in a poor light, from being exposed to a vast audience, and attracting that audience to the common cause of attacking the insurer.

This does not mean the insurer cannot justify any negative occurrence publicly and explain the corrective measures adopted, using the same media source used initially.

The need to act quickly and with transparency, besides the importance of ensuring a high satisfaction level with those to whom it relates, may lead the insurer to react to a negative comment, demonstrating why it is unfair, but despite this, adopting a measure designed to promote the well-being and satisfaction of the community, while at the same time improving the insurer's image.

The social media has the potential to generate a large number of friends and enemies in a very short time, so, regardless of how it reacts, the speed of the reaction is a very critical factor. Internal reaction processes must be prepared and planned. The technological and human resources must be in place to detect the warning signs and to implement the right reaction, in the shortest time possible.

The causes of any dissatisfaction must be carefully assessed before they turn into major issues. There are cases when contracts are cancelled or insurance premiums rise in cost on renewal by a percentage exceeding inflation that could give rise to criticism in the social media, and that has a negative impact on the insurer's image.

Social media contingencies

The social media enables *stakeholders* to express their criticisms of the insurer and to make their frustrations known, and they can do this almost immediately to a vast number of people. The reaction must be proportionate, constructive and assertive, without being humble. The risk, damage and impact of the response or non-response must be carefully assessed, bearing in mind the potential for this to blow into a public debate.

On the whole, the insurer's reaction to references must include the following:

- (where possible) contact whoever made the comment directly, or the group of people that identify with the comment;

- demonstrate how much the insurer regrets the incident and the way to overcome it in the present, and how to avoid it occurring again in the future;

- compensate the claimant with an unexpected, one-off surprise offer, leaving the same feeling warmly towards the insurer.

The final step consists of identifying the procedures, systems and people critical to the insurer's success in the social media. Indicators must be determined for each one of these variables that show the actual level of performance and the development needed to achieve the desired performance.

The metrics that monitor the presence of insurers in the social media must be known and shared, in particular:

- the variables used;

- how they are measured;

- the current values;

- the position to be achieved in 1 to 3 years.

9D) Monitoring presence in the social media

Metrics are one of the biggest marketing challenges, given the impossibility of isolating the impact of each of the variables in the specific behaviour of some customers. However, this assessment is as difficult as it is necessary. The social media demand detailed analyses to be done on returns on investment.

Measures must be defined for assessing how successful the presence of the insurer is on digital social media. Besides the metrics of each medium, there are three indicators that should be used:

- the number of new customers and sales made via the social media. This can be measured by doing a survey on those customers who adopt a certain kind of behaviour, asking them how they first came to know of the insurer. The survey determines the efficiency and effectiveness of each site in achieving the business objectives of the insurer.

- the navigation profiles of those using the insurer's social media platform, such as time spent on each page, the last pages accessed and the sites accessed after leaving the insurer's page.

- the number of reviews and assessments made by users, as well as the ratings assigned to the insurer, its insurance and to competitors. The most negative assessments are particularly important, due to the effect they have on all other users and the fact that they may suggest there is a misunderstanding that requires urgent attention.

The idea that the presence of insurers on the social media is a necessary evil is wrong. On the contrary, the social media offer the potential to gain competitive advantages over competitors. What is essential in using the social media is the ability to master their operating principles:

- understanding what the social media are, how they are organised, how they operate and what distinguishes them;

- establishing areas where the insurer wishes to remain passive (monitoring), and those where it wishes to be active (triggering initiatives and creating content);

- identifying changes and investments required to benefit from the social media, in particular technologies, systems, employee training, adaptation of processes and development of content;

If insurers manage their social media presence clearly and intelligently they will both improve their internal procedures and be ready to surprise the communities to which they belong and where they conduct their business.

Insurers need marketing that is accountable to those it attracts.

Bibliographical references

Aaker, David; Joachimsthaler, Erik (2000): *Brand Leadership: Building Assets in the Information Society*, Free Press.

Allen, Derek; Wilburn, Morris (2002): *Linking Customer and Employee Satisfaction to the Bottom Line*, ASQ.

Almaça, José António Figueiredo (1999): *El mercado ibérico de seguros*, Editorial Mapfre.

Ansoff, Igor; McDonnell, Edward (1990): *Implanting Strategic Management*, Prentice Hall, 2nd ed.

Badoc, Michel (1986): *Marketing management pour la anque et l'assurance européennes*, Les Éditions D'Organisations.

Barnes, James (2006): *Build Your Customer Strategy*, Wiley.

Barwise, Patrick; Meehan, Seán (2004): *Simply Better*, Harvard Business School Press.

Barsky, Jonathan (1999): *Finding the Profit in Customer Satisfaction*, Contemporary Books.

Bassat, Luis (1998): *El libro rojo de la publicidad*, Espasa Calpe.

Beaufre, André (2004): *Introdução à Estratégia*, Edições Sílabo.

Bernhardt, Douglas (2003): *Competitive Intelligence*, Prentice Hall.

Bhote, Keki (1996): *Beyond Customer Satisfaction to Customer Loyalty*, American Management Association.

Bickerton, Pauline; Bickerton, Mathew; Simpson-Holley, Kate (2000): *Cyberstrategy*, Butterwoth-Heinemann, 3.ª ed.

Biere, Mike (2003): *Business Intelligence for the Enterprise*, Pearson Education.

Bloching, Bjorn; Luck, Lars; Ramge, Thomas (2012): *In Data We Trust*, Bloomsbury Publishing.

Carlzon, Jan (1987): *Moments of Truth*, Ballinger Publishing Company.

Carr, Nicholas G. (2001): *The Digital Enterprise*, Harvard Business School Press.

Diacon, S.; Carter, R. (1995): *Success in Insurance*, John Murray, 3.ª ed.

Dyché, Jill (2002): *The CRM Handbook*, Addison-Wesley.

Dyer, Nigel; Watkins, Trevor (1988): *Marketing Insurance*, Kluwer Publishing, 2.ª ed.

Egan, Colin; Thomas, Michael (1998): *The CIM Handbook of Strategic Marketing,* Butterwoth-Heinemann.

Ennew, Christine; Waite, Nigel (2007): *Financial Services Marketing*, Butterwoth-Heinemann.

Ennew, Christine; Watkins, Trevor; Wright, Mike (2000): *Marketing Financial Services*, Butterwoth-Heinemann, 2.ª ed.

Evans, Liana (2010): *Social Media Marketing,* Que Publishing.

Forrester Research (2011): North American Technographics Customer Online Survey, Q4 2011.

Forsyth, Patrick (2002): *Channel Management*, Capstone Publishing.

Gabay, J. Jonathan (2000): *Successful Cyberm@rketing*, Hodder & Stoughton.

Gordon, Ian (1998): *Relationship Marketing*, Wiley.

Harrison, Tina (2000): *Financial Services Marketing,* FT Prentice Hall.

Harvard Business School Press (1991): *Strategic Marketing Management*.

Harvard Business School Press (2005): *Strategy*.

Hawkins, Del I.; Best, Roger J.; Coney, Kenneth A. (1998): *Consumer Behaviour-Building Market Strategy*, McGraw-Hill, 7.ª ed.

Hax, Arnold; Majluf, Nicolas (1996): *The Strategy Concept and Process*, Prentice-Hall, 2.ª ed.

Hill, Sam; Lederer, Chris (2001): *The Infinite Asset: Managing Brands to Build New Value*, Harvard Business School Press.

Johnson, Michael; Gustafsson, Anders (2000): *Improving Customer Satisfaction, Loyalty and Profit*, Jossey-Bass.

Kapferer, Jean-Noel (1999): *Strategic Brand Management*, Kogan Page, 2.ª ed.

Kim, W. Chan; Mauborgne, Reneé (2005): *Blue Ocean Strategy*, Harvard Business School Press.

Kirby, Justin; Marsden, Paul (2006): *Connected Marketing*, Butterworth-Heinemann.

Kotler, Philip (1999): *Kotler on Marketing*, Simon & Schuster UK Ltd.

Kotler, Philip (2003): *Marketing Management*, Prentice Hall, 11.ª ed.

Kotler, Philip; Jain, Dipak; Maesince, Suvit (2002): *Marketing Moves*, Harvard Business School Press.

Kotler, Philip; Kartajaya, Hermawan; Setiwan, Iwan (2011): *Marketing 3.0*, Atual Editora.

Kumar, V. (2008): *Managing Customers for Profit*, Wharton School Publishing.

Lambin, Jean-Jacques (1997): *Strategic Marketing Management*, McGraw-Hill.

LaSalle, Diana; Britton, Terry (2003): *Priceless,* Harvard Business School Press.

Lehmann, Donal; Winer, Russel (1997): *Analysis for Marketing Planning,* McGraw-Hill.

Lindgreen, Adam; Vanhamme, Joelle; Beverland, Michael (2009): *Memorable Customer Experiences,* Gower.

Lindon, Denis; Lendrevie, Jacques; Rodrigues, Joaquim Vicente; Dionísio, Pedro (2000): *Mercator 2000,* Publicações Dom Quixote, 9.ª ed.

Lindstrom, Martin (2008): *Buy ology,* Doubleday.

Meidan, Arthur (1984): *Insurance Marketing,* Graham Burn.

Montebello, Michel (2003): *Criação de Valor para o Cliente,* Monitor.

Moss, Larissa; Atre, Shaku (2003): *Business intelligence Roadmap,* Addison-Wesley.

Nederlof, Ad; Anton, Jon (2002): *Customer Obsession,* Anton Press, 2.ª ed.

Ofek, Elie (2002): *Customer Profitability and Lifetime Value,* Harvard Business School Press.

Parmerlee, David (2000): *Developing Successful Marketing Strategies,* NTC Business Books.

Porter, Michael E.; Kramer, Mark R. (2011): "Creating Shared Value", *Harvard Business Review,* January-February 2011, pp. 2-17.

Portugal, Luís (2007): *Gestão de Seguros Não-Vida,* IFA.

Ryals, Lynette; Knox, Simon; Maklan, Stan (2000): *Customer Relationship Management,* Prentice Hall.

Santos, António J. Robalo (2008): *Gestão Estratégica,* Escolar Editora.

Schiffman, L. G.; Kanuk, L. L. (1997): *Consumer Behaviour*, Prentice Hall, 6.ª ed.

SCN Education B.V. (2001): *Customer Relationship Management*, Vieweg.

Shaw, Colin; Dibeehi, Qaalfa; Walden, Steven (2010): *Customer Experience*, Palgrave Macmillan.

Shaw, Robert (1999): *Improving Marketing Effectiveness*, Profile Books, 2.ª ed.

Sheth, Jagdish; Eshghi, Abdolreza; Krishnan, Balaji (2011): *Internet Marketing*, Harcourt.

Siegel, Eric (2010): *Seven Reasons You Need Predictive Analytics Today*, Prediction Impact.

Sleight, Steve (2000): *Moving to E-Business*, Dorling Kindersley.

Smith, Nick; Wollan, Robert; Zhou, Catherine (2011): *The Social Media Management Handbook*, John Wiley & Sons.

Stone, Merlin; Foss, Bryan (2002): *Successful Customer Relationship Marketing*, Kogan Page.

Strauss, Judy; Frost, Raymond (2001): *E-Marketing*, Prentice Hall, 2.ª ed.

Thoyts, Rob (2010): *Insurance Theory and Practice*, Routledge.

Trepper, Charles (2000): *E-Commerce Strategies*, Microsoft Press.

Vasconcellos e Sá, Jorge Alberto (1996): *Os Senhores da Guerra*, Bertrand Editora.

Vasconcellos e Sá, Jorge Alberto (2005): *Strategy Moves*, Pearson Education.

Vilares, Manuel José; Coelho, Pedro Simões (2005): *Satisfação e Lealdade do Cliente*, Escolar Editora.

Vincent, Laurence (2012): *Brand Real*, AMACOM.

Vitale, Dona (2006): *Consumer Insights 2.0*, Paramount Market Publishing.

Walker, Orville; Boyd, Harper; Larréché, Jean-Claude (1996): *Marketing Strategy*, McGraw-Hill, 2.ª ed.

Weil, Peter; Vitale, Michael R. (2001): *Place to Space*, Harvard Business School Press.

Wilburn, Morris (2006): *Managing the Customer Experience,* ASQ.

Willcocks, Leslie; Sauer, Christopher (2000): *Moving to e-business*, Random House Business Books.

Zabin, Jeff; Brebach, Gresh (2004): *Precision Marketing,* Willey.

Zaltman, Gerald (2003): *How Customers Think*, Harvard Business School Press.

Zikmund, William; Mcleod, Raymond; Gilbert, Faye (2003): *Customer Relationship Management*, Leyh Publishing.

About the Author

Manuel Leiria holds a master's degree in Marketing Planning and Strategy and over twenty years of experience in marketing management in private and mutual insurance companies. Since 1994 has lectured Insurance Marketing and Customer Behavior courses in several post-graduate programs. Manuel Leiria is a frequent speaker at conferences about Insurance Marketing Management and Innovation.

manuel.m.leiria@gmail.com
www.insurancemarketing-thebook.com

Printed in Great Britain
by Amazon